BREAKING THE ACADEMIC LOCK STEP

Breaking the Academic Lock Step

The Development of Honors Work in American Colleges and Universities

by

FRANK AYDELOTTE

Director of the Institute for Advanced Study
Formerly President of Swarthmore College

HARPER & BROTHERS PUBLISHERS

NEW YORK AND LONDON

BREAKING THE ACADEMIC LOCK STEP

This book is complete and unabridged
in contents, and is manufactured in strict
conformity with Government regulations
for saving paper.

To the Faculty

of Swarthmore College

whose book it is

CONTENTS

PREFACE

WHEN I was invited to give the Sachs lectures at Teachers College, Columbia University, in 1939, I undertook light-heartedly to put together an account of the rapidly growing movement in American colleges and universities to provide special facilities for their abler students who are capable of going faster and further in their work than would be possible for the average. During the last twenty years this idea has swept through the country. It might be called the most important educational development of the period between the two world wars. Regimentation as to standards of work, the greatest defect of our system of higher education, hinders the development of precisely the group for which higher education does or should exist. Gradually it has come to be seen that something like the English distinction between pass and honors degrees is the solution of the problem, and hundreds of plans are based on that model.

As I set about preparing my lectures, I began to realize that the task of gathering the material would be formidable. Plans for honors work in various colleges and universities have been the subject of voluminous educational discussion, but no connected account of them has so far been written. Twenty years ago I edited for the National Research Council a report on the honors plans then in operation based upon descriptions printed in the catalogues of various colleges and universities.[1]

[1] Frank Aydelotte, editor, *Honors Courses in American Colleges and Universities,* National Research Council, 1924. (Second edition, 1925.)

Catalogue descriptions, as I know from that experience, are likely to be unsatisfactory, and questionnaires are open to still greater objection. Personal visits of inspection were called for, but making visits to a hundred and thirty colleges and universities would be the work of one or two years. Under these circumstances I raised the question with a few members of the Swarthmore faculty whether they would be willing to make these inspections, for which their own experience had so admirably prepared them. The response was instantly favorable, volunteers were called for, some thirty-five members of the faculty responded, the Carnegie Corporation generously appropriated a fund for traveling expenses, a similar grant was obtained from the General Education Board for the expense of visits to secondary schools, and during the first half of the year 1940 Swarthmore professors journeyed by rail, airplane, bus, and motor car to all parts of the country inspecting honors work. Their adventures were exciting; they received the heartiest possible welcome everywhere, and their reports to me were frank, vivid, and full of color. My necessarily tame condensation in this volume lamentably fails to do them justice. The magnitude of the task of organizing the inspections and digesting these reports compelled me to ask the Sachs Trustees for postponement of my lectures year by year from 1939 to 1942. I make my grateful acknowledgment to Dean Russell for his kindly forbearance.

No attempt is made in this volume to provide an exhaustive description of any particular plan. For that purpose an entire book would be needed for each institution. Instead only the leading features of various programs are touched upon in order to bring out points of similarity and difference and to provide a concrete basis for the discussion of the principles involved. The passage concerning each institution has been sent to some responsible officer or member of the faculty for criticism, and all statements of fact in the following pages have been approved by the institutions concerned, thus bringing the information down to the date when ordinary academic routines were displaced by the educational programs of the Army and Navy.

Nor have I attempted to describe all of the honors plans which are in successful operation. I have instead chosen those which are typical or which present some unique variation, of interest on its own account. About half of the colleges and universities visited are described in these pages; among the others are many in which honors work is equally interesting and equally successful. Four-fifths of those omitted would belong in Chapter VI. I regret not being able to include every institution about which information is available, but to try to do so would be to overload a volume which is primarily concerned with principles, and which uses the description of actual plans as illustrations and examples.

My deepest gratitude is due to my former colleagues at Swarthmore for the enthusiasm with which they gathered together the solid material upon which this study is based. My greater debt to them for the loyalty and intelligence with which they co-operated with me and with each other during the last twenty years in making a success of honors work at Swarthmore is one which can never be expressed adequately in words, but only affectionately remembered.

So ambitious a survey of honors work would have been impossible without the generous assistance of the Carnegie Corporation in providing funds to defray traveling expenses for the visits to colleges, and of the General Education Board in making a grant covering the expense of visits to secondary schools. I express my grateful appreciation to these two foundations for their gifts and for the interest which prompted them.

I am likewise under heavy obligation to the officers of the colleges and universities mentioned for their kindness in reading my descriptions of their various plans, and for giving me the benefit of their comments and corrections. I am also deeply grateful to Dr. Howard J. Savage, Secretary of the Carnegie Foundation, Dr. Henry Allen Moe, Secretary-General of the Guggenheim Foundation, to President John W. Nason and Dean Frances Blanshard of Swarthmore College, and to the Registrar of the University of Oxford and the Warden of Rhodes House for their kindness in reading my manuscript and for help with proofs. To my two secretaries, Frank Krutzke of Colorado College, who helped launch this enterprise, and Elsa Palmer Jenkins of Swarthmore, who saw it through, I am indebted for the success of what turned out to be among other things an administrative job of considerable size and complexity. Seldom has the author of a book owed so much to so many.

While the study owes its inception to the Trustees of the Sachs Lecture Fund and was made possible by grants from the Carnegie Corporation and the General Education Board, no one of these organizations has taken any responsibility for the publication of this volume, nor is to be understood as necessarily approving the statements or opinions expressed in these pages.

The same release from responsibility is due to members of the Swarthmore faculty and to professors and administrative officers of the institutions visited. It is hardly possible that in the work of condensation and interpretation I should not, in spite of the greatest pains, have fallen into errors of detail and have now and then failed to produce what either observer or observed will consider a satisfactory description of a given plan. For my sins of omission and commission I can only beg forgiveness.

As this Preface is written, many plans for honors work have had to be curtailed or suspended because of the war and the absorption of college faculties in the educational programs prescribed by the Army and Navy. The fear is sometimes expressed that accelerated and practical programs have come to stay and that work of the type here described, suspended during the war emergency, may never be resumed. Against such a danger the best defense is an offense. It has been reassuring to me to learn, from the rather extensive correspondence which has been necessary in checking descriptions of various plans, that colleges and universities all over the country are taking advantage of the suspension of normal academic work to make plans for the future in which opportunities for students of more than average ability and ambition will have an important place. It is my earnest hope that this description of such work in operation before Pearl Harbor may have value to faculty committees now engaged in the much needed task of preparing for peace by placing our liberal education on a sounder basis and by ending the regimentation which has been its greatest weakness.

FRANK AYDELOTTE

Princeton, New Jersey
September, 1943

BREAKING THE ACADEMIC LOCK STEP

CHAPTER ONE

LIBERAL EDUCATION IN THE POST-WAR WORLD

ALL times of strain, such as war or depression, tend to shake men's faith in liberal education. When danger threatens, competence to perform immediate practical tasks is at a premium and the expert takes precedence over the philosopher. Freedom of the mind then seems less useful than the habit of faithfully obeying instructions. Defense calls for efficiency. Too much emphasis on freedom of thought and the unrestricted development of the individual seems to make society less efficient, more wasteful of human resources, less manageable, less subject to planning and discipline. The miraculous achievements which flow from individual initiative and free enterprise are, when all is said, unpredictable, and do not appeal to men who, in the face of catastrophe, desire above all else to be secure. On the other hand, the very foundation of our democracy is our conception of liberal education and the freedom of the mind which that implies. Upon the broad liberal training of youth in our high schools and colleges our future will depend. This fact is widely realized and it is not surprising that men everywhere are discussing anxiously in these days the future of liberal studies.

There is another subject, however, about which men in general are even more anxious; that is security—military security, political security, and economic security. Not merely the war, but also the depression which preceded it, show how fragile is our twentieth-century civilization and how easily our supposedly inalienable rights to life, liberty, and the pursuit of happiness may be swept away. The soldiers and sailors and aviators who are fighting this war and the laborers who are supporting them at home will demand as their reward security not merely against military aggression, but also against unemployment.

There is a real conflict between these ideals. Liberal education is an adventure, both for the individual and for society: for the individual because its first aim is not to enable a man to make a living but rather to teach him how to live; for society because when able young men and women are trained to think for themselves and are left in freedom to do so, no one can predict the result. Security in war and prosperity in time of peace seem, on a superficial view, to depend more upon technical training than upon liberal knowledge.

Some degree of regimentation in war time is inevitable. Education is perforce restricted and it is the liberal element which is the first to be curtailed. That fact is strikingly illustrated by the changes brought about in American education by the present war. College students are called into military service often before their higher education is more than well begun. For those that remain programs must be altered in accordance with military needs. In the curricula prescribed by the Army and Navy there is and must be strong emphasis upon technical subjects at the expense of liberal studies and this fact has aroused widespread apprehension as to the future of the liberal college. The cruel test of war brings out in sharp relief what seem to be the manifold inefficiencies of liberal education.

This is a war of physicists and engineers. The day has gone by when it was sufficient training for a soldier to teach him to shoot straight with a rifle and lunge effectively with a bayonet, to develop his physical strength and courage, and to give him the discipline needed to make him behave well in combat. The soldier of today must learn to handle intelligently many kinds of intricate mechanical devices. He must be a specialist in the operation of tanks, airplanes, artillery, radio, and other precision instruments of great complexity. He needs at least an elementary understanding of mathematics, physics, navigation, meteorology, and other scientific subjects. The training of soldiers and sailors demands vast schemes of practical scientific and mechanical instruction.

The manufacture of the implements of war likewise calls into play all the resources of our physicists, chemists, engineers, inventors, and skilled mechanics, and all the resources of industrial management. Never before in history have we had so close a relationship between abstruse theoretical research by the physicist in his laboratory, scientific mass production of heretofore unprecedented accuracy, and practical use of scientific instruments of warfare on the battle field, on the high seas, and in the air above. Our strength in battle seems to depend not so much on broad liberal education as upon highly specialized technical skill.

The question has arisen in many minds whether the post-war period, which will confront us with a different though no less severe test, may not produce a similar demand for the revamping of our entire educational program along more practical lines. In the first place all the accelerated scientific discoveries and mechanical improvements made under the stimulus of war will contribute to the amelioration of human life in time of peace. Nothing is more fascinating than the romantic predictions, which sound like fairy tales but which will doubtless some day be sober reality, of the marvelous gadgets we shall all have to play with when the war is over and we are able once again to beat our scientific swords into mechanized and automatic ploughshares. There will be no end to the wonderful toys and useful tools which we shall make out of the newly developed instruments of war—tanks, battle planes, radio equipment, new alloys, and plastics. Health will be improved and sickness eased by new discoveries in connection with nutrition and newly developed medical and surgical techniques. All of these contributions to human welfare depend upon science and technology and will inevitably enhance the importance of technical training in the post-war world.

In the second place there are signs which point to a parallel enhancement of the importance of the techniques of the social sciences, especially economics. The last quarter of a century has been a period of daring economic experimentation in many countries. War and depression have revolutionized traditional methods in public finance and private trade. Economic problems—unemployment, social security, international trade and finance—have become increasingly technical and complex. They are in many respects too difficult for the layman and tax the knowledge of the expert. The so-called brain trust is the logical answer. Governments and large industrial organizations depend more and more upon expert knowledge in the fields of trade and finance just as they have done in the past in the field of public health.

The war has witnessed for the first time in history the mobilization of the total economic strength of all the great nations engaged, at the price, for the most part willingly paid, of national regimentation and the substitution of specialized technical training for broad liberal education. The question inevitably arises whether this strength cannot similarly be mobilized for the purpose of realizing peaceful ends, to free the world from want, and whether if this is done it will not demand similar regimentation and similar emphasis upon technical skill at the expense of liberal values.

It is such considerations as these which cause men to fear that this war may mark a turning point in the development of our system of higher education, away from the liberal arts to technical training of experts in the natural and social sciences. Men fear that nations and individuals in the post-war world will be so poor, will feel so insecure, that they will be compelled to study how to get a living at the expense of how to live. The demand for security—economic security, political security, and what one might call ideological security—will be strong in this and every other country. We shall be in danger, in the search for security, of curtailing the life of freedom and adventure which is the condition of all high achievement. It is not only in the sphere of politics and international relations that timidity is fatal and "security mortal's chiefest enemy." It may be also that weariness and want will make men and nations fearful of freedom of economic enterprise, freedom of scientific invention, and freedom of speculation in the realm of pure intellect. Regimentation of the human spirit in one direction may lead to its regimentation in all forms of activity.

As has been said, a certain degree of regimentation in war time is necessary and inevitable. The present college generation must sacrifice liberal education in order to learn the technique of war. To that extent we give up what we are fighting for in order to defend it. No one will complain of the sacrifice if it is only temporary. But regimentation for the sake of security after the war is another matter. We may expect that the demand for it will be formidable and meeting that demand will be the real test of the firmness with which we hold to our educational and spiritual ideals.

One cannot but feel that such a shift in emphasis in our education would be a moral and spiritual calamity, that no measure, however full, of material comfort and security would justify. Even if human life has been insecure—solitary, nasty, poor, brutish, and short, it has been better than the life of Leacock's man in asbestos. To abandon the ideals of liberal education would mean that in winning the war we had given up all that we are fighting for and it would be furthermore a tragic misreading of the lesson which we ought to learn from the issue of the conflict. This war is a contest between individualism and totalitarianism. And just as freedom and individualism, despite a late start and despite many errors and inefficiencies, are now beginning to show themselves strong enough to prevail in the struggle, we may hope that they will be strong enough to prevail in the post-war world. We must not allow ourselves to forget that freedom—political freedom and freedom of the mind—has been our greatest asset in the present war. The totalitarian powers had a long start in technical preparation. What they do not have and cannot develop is the courage which free men show in meeting adversity and in struggling against odds. The problems of the war and of the peace are fundamentally not technical but moral, philosophical, and religious. They can be solved only by men into whose education has been infused a liberal element which makes the man so trained not a mere tool ready to be turned to the service of any power above him, ready to do his job regardless of whether the consequences of his work are good or evil, but rather a thinking being, a citizen, morally responsible, who will take into consideration not merely means but also ends.

It is upon these considerations that we are entitled, in my opinion, to put our faith in the continuity of the liberal tradition. No abstruse arguments will be needed to drive home that point. The lesson will be plain for all to read. We may even expect in the enthusiasm of victory a reaction in the direction of those liberal studies which alone can give victory its true meaning and guide us in the building of the brave new world of our dreams. It is not without significance for the future that many college professors find that their Army and Navy students are keenly interested in those liberal subjects which have been included in the military curriculum. But this is not the time for those of us who believe passionately in the value of liberal studies to be complacent. It is rather a time to examine critically our whole plan for liberal education, to define our aims, to abolish the wasteful and stupid routines which are sometimes the product of traditional methods too long continued, and to avoid, on the other hand, the fads and aberrations into which men fall in the mistaken belief that any change is an improvement.

If our liberal education is to meet the needs of the post-war world we must clarify its aims and improve its quality. Energetic and effective efforts to do both have been the most encouraging fact of our educational situation during the last twenty years. As to aims, it is already becoming clear that the central purpose of liberal education cannot be restricted to the study of any particular subject or combination of subjects. It is not a problem of requiring every student to take courses in Latin and Greek. Nor is it a problem of resisting the claims of science, which for students with any aptitude for it must be an important ingredient in the liberal education of the future. Liberal knowledge is not a formula; it is a point of view.

The essence of liberal education is the development of mental power and moral responsibility in each individual. It is based upon the theory that each person is unique, that each deserves to have his own powers developed to the fullest possible extent—his intellect, his character, and his sensitiveness to beauty—as over against merely learning some useful technique.

There is no such sharp distinction between liberal education and technical education as prejudice, even learned prejudice, sometimes believes. Instruction in the plays of Shakespeare may be strictly technical, while electrical engineering or law may be liberal, according to the point of view from which each is studied. An educational system based on belief in the value of liberal knowledge will infuse a liberal element into all training, even the most technical, while exclusive preoccupation with techniques, with means as opposed to ends, may deprive the study of literature, or philosophy, or history, or religion, of any liberal element.

When peace comes the need for making the most of our best brains for the service of democracy will be not less but more insistent than ever. The tasks which will confront this and every country will be unprecedented in their difficulty and importance, and in the performance of these tasks we shall have to face the choice between regimentation and the voluntary efforts of free men and women. We must choose between the calculable but mediocre results of planning imposed from without and the brilliant but incalculable results of individual initiative working in freedom.

Only our best brains and our highest idealism, trained in freedom and working in freedom, can solve the appalling economic and political problems which we shall face. The democracies have for a long time failed to build into their institutions of government and industry the best ideas of their ablest thinkers. They have not always done so even in education. They must do so in every department of the democratic way of life, if that life is to persist. No merely defensive attitude will meet the need. Only by a democratic attack, world-wide in scope, as daring as are the dreams of the dictators, upon the evils of ignorance and selfishness and want, can the world be made a fit place to live in. Such an attack must involve the public spirit which places the common welfare above private ends in time of peace, as men so naturally do in time of war. It must be as intelligent as campaigns of conquest are stupid. Its aim must be to utilize the resources of nature and the achievements of science to raise the standard of living, material and spiritual, everywhere, and to utilize the resources of intelligence and good will to deal justly with all men and nations. Civilization in one country or one part of the world is meaningless unless its aim is to make all men civilized. Modern industry has unified the world, modern science has made all men neighbors, and we are false to all our ideals unless we treat them as such. This war will mark the beginning of a new and better age than we have ever had before or it will mark the beginning of the end of our civilization.

Only by education can we translate into practice the great aims for which we have been fighting. Those aims are in the last analysis intellectual and spiritual. They can never be realized by the mere mastery of scientific and engineering and economic techniques. They can never be realized by turning men into machines, even though food, clothing, shelter, and amusements are guaranteed.

If we strive, as we must, to realize these high aims, we can do so only by improving the quality of the liberal education offered in our high schools and colleges. The greatest defect of that education is the regimentation of individuals of different levels of ability into the same program. We offer to our students in high school and college bewildering freedom as to the subjects they should study. But once they have made their choice we set up a common standard of achievement for the poorest, the average, and the best. The converse of this policy would produce better results. With some knowledge of the ambitions and aptitudes of a given individual, older heads may well be wiser as to the subjects which he should study. But once the plan of study is determined it is obvious that each individual should be required to come up to the highest standard of excellence of which he is capable. This can never be the case if individuals of all levels of ability are taught in the same classes and set the same examinations. That is the common practice. It constitutes a kind of academic lock step, bad for the poorest and wasteful for the best. We must eliminate that waste if we are to have a liberal training adequate to the needs of the post-war world. While seeing to it that individuals of each level of ability have the training best suited to them, we must realize that the future of our country depends upon what happens to the best. It is from the ablest young men and women, given the proper training, that we may hope for the leadership without which democracy cannot survive.

The immense increase in the enrollment in high schools and colleges at the end of the last war first made educators generally aware of the vast range of individual differences. As a result, during the last twenty years energetic and promising measures have been taken to make education individual and selective. Following the example of the English universities, whose greatest contribution to democratic education is a workable solution of this problem, most of the leading colleges and universities of the United States have put into operation programs for students of unusual ability and ambition which, instead of holding them back to the average pace, allow them to go forward as far and as fast as they can. The description and discussion of these plans constitute the subject matter of this volume. No one would say that they are as yet perfectly worked out or satisfactory in all details. But they make a good beginning, upon which it is to be hoped plans for higher education after this war will be based.

It requires courage in a democracy like ours, which considers each man as good as his neighbor, if not a little better, to put into operation what seems to many an aristocratic method of education. But we must learn to see the error in that superficial interpretation of democracy which assumes that all men are equal in intellectual ability. We must understand that in recognizing individual differences we are paying the truest homage to the worth of all individuals. Universities and colleges and schools which are today facing the problem of giving to undergraduates of each level of ability opportunities suited to their needs are fulfilling their function in our democracy. They are keeping up their communications with the future. They are ensuring the training of citizens who can make their greatest contribution to all the offices of peace and war, whether as loyal followers or as leaders of courage and insight. The ideal for democratic education good enough to meet the needs of the post-war world must be not security but excellence.

Chapter Two

THE ACADEMIC LOCK STEP

AMERICAN students are as individuals extraordinarily free. They have their own self-government associations, they manage their own college activities, they take almost complete responsibility for their personal conduct. But the methods of mass education, which are all but universal even in small colleges, effectively deny them the opportunity of taking the same kind of responsibility for their intellectual development. The system of instruction which forms the subject of this book might be described as an extension of undergraduate freedom from the personal to the intellectual sphere. It is essentially a system for selecting the best and most ambitious students, prescribing for these students a more severe program than would be possible for the average, and allowing them freedom and opportunity to work out that program for themselves.

The instruction of the average American student has been standardized beyond the point where uniformity has value. This is perhaps the natural result of the immense increase in numbers of college students during the last half-century. We have in our colleges and universities as many students as we had in the high schools two generations ago. The standardization of the instruction of these masses has been carried to a point where it resembles the Federal Reserve system. If a student has a certain number of hours of academic credit in a certain recognized college, he can cash in this credit at any other recognized college just as he might cash a check through a Federal Reserve bank. Intellectual values cannot be correctly represented by this system.

The system assumes that all college students are substantially alike, that all subjects are equal in educational value, that all instruction in institutions of a certain grade is approximately equal in effectiveness, and that when a student has accumulated a certain specified number of credit hours he has a liberal education. All these assumptions are of course false. All courses of instruction are not equally effective; all subjects are not equal in educational value; our students are extraordinarily different in their interests and intellectual capacity; and it is only by qualitative, not quantitative, standards that liberal knowledge can be recognized and measured.

Our ordinary academic system is planned to meet the needs of that hypothetical individual—the average student. It does not pay him the compliment of assuming that his ability is very great or that he has any consuming interest in his studies. Its purpose is to make sure that he does a certain amount of carefully specified routine work. He can get a degree without undergoing any profound intellectual transformation; he can even get a degree without doing much work; but he cannot escape conformity to a prescribed academic routine. He must faithfully attend classes, hand in themes and exercises, undergo frequent tests and quizzes, follow instructions, and obey regulations, which are the same for all. He is treated not as an individual, but as a member of a group. It is felt to be essential that every undergraduate should attend from twelve to fifteen classes each week and that he should spend from one to two hours in study or in doing exercises in preparation for each class. All this is based on the assumption that if it takes one student two hours to read a certain number of pages of his textbook or to write a theme or solve a set of problems, it will take every other about the same amount of time.

In Chapter V I discuss the question whether the system is a bad one for the average college student. It may be argued that it has demonstrated its value as a preparation for business and for many other occupations, and that it takes care of the average man adequately if not ideally. Certainly the harm it does is mainly to the best and the most ambitious. We have in every college and university a smaller or larger group who are capable of going faster than the average, who do not need the routine exercises which are necessary for those of mediocre ability, who do not need the prodding which is necessary for those who possess no real intellectual interests. The academic system as ordinarily administered is for these better and more ambitious students a kind of lock step: it holds them back, wastes their time, and blunts their interest by subjecting them to a slow-moving routine which they do not need. It causes, furthermore, the atrophy of the qualities of independence and initiative in more gifted individuals by furnishing too little opportunity for their exercise.

Our college activities are organized on a different theory. Whereas in studies the virtue most in demand is docility, in extra-curricular clubs, teams, and societies the undergraduate has a chance to plan for himself, to exercise his own initiative, to succeed or fail on his own responsibility. It is not surprising that many students feel that they get the best part of their education outside the classroom and that employers often look more keenly at the young graduate's record in activities than they do at his grades. Docility has its uses but independence and initiative are virtues of a higher order. The man who will do what he is told at the time he is told to do it has a certain value in the world, but the man who will do it without being told is worth much more. Consequently when one faces the problem of providing a more severe course of instruction for our abler students, one sees immediately that it is not sufficient merely to provide more of the same kind of work. The work must be different; it must not only be harder but must also offer more freedom and responsibility, more scope for the development of intellectual independence and initiative.

The English universities have long ago faced and solved this problem. They make a frank distinction between those students who are interested in the intellectual life and those who are not. They give the mediocre student a degree on easier terms than we do, but they require of those who are intellectually ambitious a more severe standard than we have ever, until recently, dared to require; and they give to those students more freedom in working out their education than we have ever dared to give. They do not tell the honors man what he must do in order to get an education; they tell him what he must know. Their requirements are expressed in terms of the examinations he must pass. There is a sound basis for all of this. Our academic requirements are too much concerned with processes, assuming that if the student goes through the motions, he will get an education.

We must break the lock step of the course and hour system if we are to give our students of varying levels of ability a training which will develop adequately the powers of each. The free elective system and the profusion of courses offered give each individual an embarrassing range of choice as to what he shall study. But the amount and difficulty of the work required in each course are rigidly standardized to the capacity of the average. It is not feasible to fail more than a small proportion of the members of each class, and this fact effectively limits the difficulty of the work required to what all or nearly all can do. The assignments or reading must not exceed in character or amount the capacity and interests of the student of average ability. The lectures and class discussions must not be over his head. The result is that the student of unusual ability suffers in many ways: he may become an idler, or he may devote his spare time to a wide variety of extra-curricular activities on which he tends to set an entirely fictitious value. In too many cases, comparing himself with his duller colleagues, he tends to rate too highly his own ability and achievements.

The student who is below the average standard, on the other hand, becomes discouraged and disheartened in the vain attempt to perform tasks which are too much for him. For a longer or shorter time he drags along, looking eagerly for easy courses, seeking help from private tutors, trying to catch up by attending summer schools, endeavoring by expedients which are sometimes pathetic and sometimes heroic to gain the coveted A.B. degree. A few succeed, but many are forced to confess themselves failures and to drop out, which is partly the reason why in many universities not more than one-fourth of the entering freshmen are able to graduate with their class. If one thinks in terms of education and not merely of the degree, it is obvious that the solution for both groups is to set them tasks adjusted to their mental capacity, their previous preparation, and their intellectual interests.

The problem in this acute form is one of recent decades. Fifty years ago when President Eliot was proposing the elective system at Harvard, the level of ability of American students was much more uniform. Colleges and universities were smaller, enrollment was limited by financial considerations and by the fact that for many careers a college education was not thought to be the best preparation. Gradually all this has changed. Scholarships (awarded often on the basis of need rather than ability) and a thousand forms of self-help have placed a college education within the reach of practically any determined boy or girl; and, as might be expected, a good many of those who show least aptitude for the abstract studies upon which the college degree depends, are cleverest and most resourceful in meeting the practical concrete problems of earning their living and paying their college bills.

Meanwhile, college experience, if not a college degree, has become a requirement for many white-collar occupations. The result has been that in the last fifty years the number of college students in the United States has grown by leaps and bounds. In that period the number of colleges and universities in the country has been more than doubled, the number of students has been multiplied by twenty, and the combined budgets of our institutions of higher education multiplied by a factor of forty or fifty. We are giving higher education, not merely to larger number, but also to a greater proportion of our young people of college age than any country in the world has ever tried to do before.[1]

With this stupendous increase in numbers has come a much wider range of levels of ability. Fifty years ago the limitations set by custom and interest upon entrance to college produced a student group of much more homogeneous character. Now our undergraduates are a cross section of the nation. It was only when the number of college students increased so remarkably at the end of the last war that the menace to standards began to be widely recognized.

By that time we were faced not merely with the difficulty of the average versus the superior student, but also with a

[1] W. S. Learned, in *The Quality of the Educational Process in the United States and Europe* (Carnegie Foundation, Bulletin No. 20, 1927), gives on page 114 an approximate tabulation of the numbers. According to Learned's figures three times as many men between the ages of 20 and 24 attend higher institutions in the United States as in France, Germany or Great Britain, and five or six times as many of both sexes combined. Dr. Learned's *Bulletin* is a stimulating discussion of the problem considered in this chapter.

large and increasing group for whom even the average standard was too high. In the state universities, to which any high-school graduate must be admitted on the basis of his diploma, and in many small colleges where need for students prevents the enforcement of any higher qualification for entrance, the standards of the average are beginning to be pulled down by the students who are below the average in ability or preparation. The number of these below-average students (roughly speaking those who graduate in the lower half of their class in high school) is constantly on the increase. These students are frequently not adapted to the subjects included in the ordinary program of study and they cannot keep up with the level of achievement of the average college student, modest as is that standard. They deserve nevertheless that their needs should be understood and met. It is important that the subjects they study be suited to their interests and that they should not learn to think of themselves as failures simply because they are set to perform tasks in which they are not interested and to which they are not equal. It is still more important that, just as the average student should not be allowed to pull down the level of the best, so these below-average individuals should not be allowed to become a threat to the standards of work of the average. Taken all in all, the variation in levels of ability of our undergraduates is the most serious problem confronting American higher education today.

The importance of the problem is widely realized. Practically all of the best American colleges and universities are taking steps to meet it. The measures they adopt are varied and are by no means equally successful. Reforms are hindered by academic conservatism and timidity, by vested interests of student organizations and departments, and by a vast system of extra-curricular activities which have rushed into the intellectual vacuum created by our conventional academic system.

The most serious of these hindrances is the confusion of thought inherent in our theories of democracy. To many people democracy means equality, and equality means uniformity. Our people wear the same clothes, eat the same food, drive the same cars, see the same movies, listen to the same radio programs. Why should they not have the same education? The fact that we do not all do the same kind of work, read the same books, look at the same paintings, or listen to the same music is for the moment forgotten. It is also forgotten that one of the purposes of democracy is to provide each individual with the opportunity that is best for him and that our society needs services of increasing variety and complexity. The end of democracy should be not to make men uniform, but rather to give them freedom to be individuals.

The confusion in the aims of democracy between uniformity and individualism comes home with special force to education, and it may well be that our colleges and universities, in solving the problem of the best treatment for students of different levels of ability, will contribute something to the solution of one of the central problems of the democratic way of life. We must guard against the temptation to think that a man's worth as an individual or his value to society can be measured by his aptitude for mathematics or languages. We must recognize that there are diversities of gifts, but whether it be plumbing or Plato that is in question, a society that is not to be condemned to mediocrity must demand the best of each.

CHAPTER THREE

PASS AND HONORS DEGREES AT OXFORD

⎧WITHOUT educational theorizing and without apparent design, the universities of Oxford and Cambridge developed more than a century ago a workable solution of the problem which I stated in the preceding chapter.⎭ It is not surprising that in this respect we should have much to learn from them. What we call the college of liberal arts is an Anglo-Saxon institution. In the development of an undergraduate course, leading to the B.A. degree, designed to provide a liberal education, the English universities have had a longer experience than ours and their example has much to teach us. That example has, during the last forty years, largely as a result of the Rhodes Scholarships, been brought strongly to the attention of American educational authorities, and English methods have come to rival those of the German universities in their effect upon American higher education.

⎧At Oxford the B.A. degree is granted on the basis of examinations plus a minimum requirement of residence.⎭ There are no courses or credits. Instruction is by the method of individual tutorials, and by laboratory work in the sciences, supplemented by lectures, attendance at which is largely voluntary. A tutor will warn his students against attending too many lectures; he may advise sampling several at the beginning of term and continuing only with one or two which seem most interesting or useful. A student is expected to work mainly by himself. Vacations are long and are utilized by the most ambitious undergraduates for harder and more concentrated work than is possible in term time.

Aside from Responsions, which must be passed for entrance, two examinations are required for the Oxford B.A. degree: an intermediate examination, Moderations or some one of its various equivalents, taken sometime during the first or second year, designed to demonstrate the candidate's fitness for advanced work; and a final examination for the degree. Both the intermediate examination and the final are given in two forms, pass and honors. If a candidate aspires to honors both in the intermediate examination and in finals, he will ordinarily need four years for his university course. If, as is often done, he takes the intermediate examination in the pass form, he need devote but one year or even less to preparation for that examination and can take either the pass or the honors degree at the end of three years. A certain leeway is granted as to when a student should present himself for a given examination. This amounts in some cases to as much as a year, and the decision rests with the student, acting upon the advice of his tutor, as to whether he shall take a longer or shorter time in preparation, and whether his university course shall extend over three years, or four.

The difference in standard between the pass and honors examinations is considerable. The one covers more ground than the other and an entirely different quality of thought is demanded. Probably an Oxford pass degree can be obtained on easier terms than could the B.A. degree in any approved American college or university. On the other hand, the standard for the honors degree at Oxford is higher, both in quantity of work done and in quality, than the conventional requirements of the best American colleges.

The requirements for these various examinations are outlined, not in terms of courses which the student must take, but rather in terms of the topics and subjects which he is expected to master. He is told not what he must do but what he is expected to know.)The volume which corresponds most nearly to the catalogue of an American college or university is the *Examination Statutes*, a kind of syllabus or outline of the subject matter tested in each of the examinations conducted by the University.)Subjects are listed, set books or topics are specified, indications are given as to which papers are required of all candidates and which ones may be offered voluntarily. The *Examination Statutes* is a handbook alike for the student in planning his course, for his tutor who is aiding and advising him, and for the examiner who will pronounce upon the merits of his work.[1]

(The honors degree is practically required for all students who aspire to an intellectual career. A pass degree may suffice for a schoolmastership (especially if accompanied by marked ability in sports), or for a career in business. For any of the learned professions or for a career in the civil service, or for any occupation of similar quality, an honors degree is necessary.) All scholarship holders are expected as a matter of course to be candidates for honors, as are Rhodes Scholars, unless they are prepared to embark at once on work for one of the higher research degrees.)For the honors man the class received (first, second, third, or fourth) is extremely important. A first sends him off on his career in life with a flying start; a third may make it advisable for him to alter his plans and enter some less ambitious occupation.)For this reason it

[1] Fuller details of the organization of Oxford honor schools may be obtained from the *Oxford University Handbook* and the *Examination Statutes*, both published by the Oxford University Press. A shorter account, written from the American point of view, will be found in *Oxford of Today*, edited by Crosby, Aydelotte, and Valentine, Oxford Press, American Branch, 1922. (Second edition, 1927.)

is well worth while for the man who is not sure of his preparation, or who may not have made the best possible use of his time at Oxford or in his vacations, to take an extra year before presenting himself for the final honors examinations in order to obtain a better class.

(The oldest and most famous honors school at Oxford is *Literae Humaniores*, commonly known as Greats.) If the value of an intellectual discipline may be judged by the eminence of the careers of the men trained in it, there is good ground for the assertion that Greats has for a century stood first in the entire university world. (Its pre-eminent value is commonly attributed to the superiority of the Greek and Latin classics as training for the mind and to the severity of the standard which has prevailed in this School.) It can, however, be maintained that the Greats School owes as much of its value to its breadth as to its content. It is not confined to the study of Greek and Latin literature: indeed the purely literary part of the course is mainly restricted to Honor Moderations, the intermediate examination which normally prepares for it. The final examinations for the degree in *Literae Humaniores* include the great periods of ancient history and philosophy with appropriate modern comment.) The school embraces the whole of ancient civilization and its impact on modern thought. Adequate preparation for success in so exacting a test must begin with a solid foundation in preparatory school and continue throughout the entire university course. Such prolonged specialization, however, is not narrowing because of the character of the subjects included and because of the broad way in which by tradition this material is treated. (The requirement for success is twofold: exact knowledge of certain set books and topics, coupled with capacity to deal in broad generalities with a wide range of historical and literary material.)

The training offered by honors in classics at Oxford has been valuable not merely for a literary or scholarly career. It has also been the training of English statesmen, colonial administrators, military leaders, and business men; (it has proved its value for every office of peace and war.) Its popularity is not now so great as it was fifty years ago; modern literature and the natural and social sciences attract many students who formerly would have studied the classics, but probably most Oxford Dons would still consider Greats to be the most rigorous and the most valuable training which Oxford has to offer.

In a preceding paragraph I have raised the question whether the success of *Literae Humaniores* is not due more to the breadth and to the admirable organization of the School than to the pre-eminence of the ancient classics as material for literary education.(Some of the newer honor schools at Oxford —English and the modern languages, for example—are by comparison quite narrowly specialized, and tend to confine the student to literary topics, omitting the elements of history and philosophy. The only important exception is the school of Philosophy, Politics, and Economics, the so-called Modern Greats,) established immediately after the last war, which includes a similarly broad range of subjects in the modern field.) The success of Modern Greats seems to me to prove the soundness of the theory on which it was organized and I believe that the study of English and other modern literatures, and of the natural sciences, might be improved in value if they included a broader range.[2] There has been for some time discussion of a possible honor school of science and

[2] There is a fuller discussion of the point in Chapter V of Frank Aydelotte's *The Oxford Stamp*, Oxford University Press, American Branch, 1917, and in a commentary, "Oxford's Opportunity" by. J. St. Loe Strachey, in the *Spectator* for July 27, 1918, p. 87.

philosophy at Oxford but no program has yet been suggested which could command the support of the faculties concerned.

When a century ago (in 1830) the honors examinations were definitely separated from the examinations for the pass degree at Oxford, the number of candidates for honors was small and the great majority of the students took the ordinary degree. The first statute, thirty years earlier, providing for honors and class lists, had limited the number of candidates in any one year to twelve, and in 1809 Brasenose College with three candidates monopolized all the First Classes. Gradually over the years the number of candidates for honors has increased and the number of pass men declined.

The colleges were, of course, particularly interested in the type of man who would be able to qualify for honors. Gradually a few colleges came to make candidacy for honors a requirement for admission. The custom has spread until today most of the colleges at Oxford insist that their undergraduates shall read for honors and only a few are willing to admit pass men. The number of pass men is steadily decreasing and is now about 100 in a normal undergraduate body of over 4000. It may easily be that the pass degree will in a few more years disappear entirely, though it is a question whether such a development would be fortunate. The same arguments which made the introduction of the honors degree into American universities so desirable would favor the retention of the pass degree at Oxford. The standard in any examination is influenced inevitably by the average capacity of the men who take it. If all undergraduates are required to read for honors it would seem difficult to keep the honors standard as high as could be done if there were a pass course into which those men could be put (and indeed would be glad to go) who in their first year did not show promise of being able to come up to the standard of honors work.

(The history of the development of the honor schools at Oxford and the differentiation between the honors and the pass degree has particular significance for American colleges and universities because the problems of British and American higher education are so similar.) At the end of the nineteenth century American universities were deeply influenced by German methods. We owe more to German standards of scholarship than we are in war time willing to acknowledge. But in certain respects German methods are not applicable to American conditions. German universities, indeed all universities outside English-speaking countries, are postgraduate schools. (The undergraduate college of liberal arts exists only in the United States, Great Britain, and the states of the British Commonwealth.) Cardinal Newman's classic definition of liberal knowledge, *The Idea of a University*, applies only to universities in the English-speaking world.) It is not surprising that American universities, where the undergraduate problem is the most important one, should have much to learn from the English universities which have had the longest and most successful experience with this problem.

(Universities of the continental type place more emphasis on the training of the specialist; those of the Anglo-Saxon type emphasize more strongly the ideal of liberal education.) The question is one of emphasis; neither type excludes the aims of the other.) The German gymnasium and the French lycée offer a liberal education of high quality and are famous for the severity of their standards; the American graduate and professional schools offer thorough and highly specialized training based upon the foundation of the work done in the college of liberal arts. Nevertheless, the difference of emphasis is real, important, and characteristic.

(Other things being equal, the Anglo-Saxon type of education seems better suited to the purposes of democracy; the

continental type to an authoritarian regime.) It is possible
under either system to produce the specialist who is not
interested in the great ends of society, whose first concern
is not moral values, who stands ready to do the task he is
trained to do whether the results tend to the upbuilding of
society or to its destruction.) Such men may be produced by
either system but it would seem easier to produce them under
the continental system than under the Anglo-Saxon.

On the other hand, it is possible to train under either system
the man who is a citizen first and a technician second, who
insists upon thinking for himself about the significance of the
work he is called upon to do, who will place public welfare
above private success. Such men are produced under both
systems but it would seem that the Anglo-Saxon university,
with its increased amount of time devoted to liberal training,
would offer a more congenial environment in which these
qualities could develop.(Certainly our common heritage of
democracy makes it important that we in the United States
should seek to learn all that we can from the English educational system.)

The establishment of the Rhodes Scholarships in 1904 had
the effect of calling the attention of American colleges and
universities to the importance of English experience.(Whatever subject a Rhodes Scholar may study at Oxford, he studies
also inevitably English methods of higher education.[3] There
are now over one thousand ex-Rhodes Scholars in the United
States and another five hundred Americans who went to
Oxford or Cambridge on their own account. Approximately
one-third of these men have become college and university
teachers and administrators. They naturally seek to apply at
home the best of what they learned in England. What they

[3] In this connection see Frank Aydelotte, "What the American Rhodes
Scholar Gets from Oxford," *Scribner's*, June, 1923.

have written about English methods has attracted the attention
of many wide-awake American university men, who themselves have never studied at Oxford. The result has been the
adaptation to American conditions of many of the methods
of English higher education. The tutorial system, always used
to a certain extent in American colleges, has become much
more widespread. Comprehensive examinations have come in
to supplement or supplant the fragmentary course examinations of the conventional American type. The division of
Oxford and Cambridge into colleges has now been introduced
at Harvard and Yale and Claremont and in a few other American universities. Most important of all, the distinction between the pass and honors degrees has been adopted, in
principle at least, in nearly three-fourths of all the colleges
and universities included in the list approved by the Association of American Universities.[4] The idea is spreading rapidly
and seems likely to continue to spread. As put into practice
it is not a mere slavish imitation of Oxford methods, but
rather the adaptation of a principle to American conditions,
to the solution of an American problem. It is the purpose of
this volume to describe and discuss the various ways in which
this principle of special provision for superior students has
been woven into the American academic system.

Cecil Rhodes took a pass degree at Oxford. Even that was
for him rather a heroic feat. His health made it impossible
for him to live for any long period in the English climate.
Instead he came to and fro from South Africa carrying on
his business and his studies at Oxford intermittently as do
many American undergraduates at the present time. However modest his own attainments, Rhodes had a deep and

[4] For fuller discussion of this point see Frank Aydelotte, "Progress of
the American College in Two Decades: In Intellectual Achievement,"
Bulletin of the Association of American Colleges, XXX, 1, March, 1935.

lifelong respect for learning, and we may believe that it would give him satisfaction to know that one important result of his scholarships has been to bring about a notable improvement in the standards of undergraduate work in this country.

CHAPTER FOUR

THE SWARTHMORE PLAN

WHEN I went to Swarthmore as President in 1921 I was seeking an opportunity to try out the ideas outlined in the two preceding chapters. In my interviews with members of the Board of Managers before my appointment I explained my purpose at length. I thought I saw from the response which greeted my ideas that Swarthmore offered a favorable opportunity for such an experiment. To make assurance doubly sure, I requested the permission of the Board, after I had been formally offered the presidency, to interview the leading members of the faculty. To these individuals I repeated my concern, and the cordiality with which my ideas were received determined me to accept.

At the time I knew little about Quakerism, but I quickly realized without being told that the Quakers, from having always been a minority group, had formed the habit of considering ideas on their merits and did not think that a point of view was necessarily sound because it was held by the majority. In this I was right and I am sure that the Quaker tradition of Swarthmore contributed more than anyone, even the Quakers themselves, realized to the success of honors work.

I outlined my purposes in becoming a college president in the following paragraphs of my inaugural address, which at the suggestion of Raymond Walters, who was then Dean, were for many years printed in the opening pages of the catalogue:

Perhaps the most fundamentally wasteful feature of our educational institutions is the lack of a higher standard of intellectual attainment. We are educating more students up to a fair average than any country in the world, but we are wastefully allowing the capacity of the average to prevent us from bringing the best up to the standard they could reach. Our most important task at present is to check this waste.

The method of doing it seems clear: To separate those students who are really interested in the intellectual life from those who are not, and to demand of the former in the course of their four years' work, a standard of attainment for the A.B. degree distinctly higher than we require of them at present and comparable perhaps with that which is now reached for the A.M.

I do not believe that we should deny to the average, or below average student, the benefit of a college education. He needs this training, and we need his humanizing presence in the colleges, but we should not allow him to hold back his more brilliant companions from doing that high quality of work which will in the end best justify the time and money which we spend in education.

With these more brilliant students it would be possible to do things which we dare not attempt with the average. We could allow them to specialize more because their own alertness of mind would of itself be sufficient to widen their intellectual range and give them that acquaintance with other studies necessary for a liberal point of view. We could, I think, at least partially obliterate the distinction between vocational and liberal studies. This is strikingly true in such a subject as engineering where the brilliant student can dispense with a great many of the detailed technical applications of scientific knowledge because his very power of reasoning enables him to apply fundamental principles to detailed situations. The time thus saved could be used for the development of general intelligence through liberal studies in such a way as to turn out in the same length of time that we are now giving to engineering courses, men who would be at once more fundamentally trained in their subject and more broadly educated.)

We could give these more brilliant students greater independence in their work, avoiding the spoon-feeding which makes much of our college instruction of the present day of secondary-school character. Our examinations should be less frequent and more comprehensive, and the task of the student should be to prepare himself for these tests through his own reading and through the instruction offered by the College: he should not be subjected to the petty, detailed, day-by-day restrictions and assignments necessary for his less able fellows.[1]

A few weeks after my inauguration, as I was engaged in the multifarious duties of a new college president trying to learn his job, studying budgets and academic requirements, looking into student activities and athletics, listening to complaints about college meals and dormitory furniture, making speeches to alumni, and trying to do justice to Philadelphia hospitality, I was waited upon by a committee of the Swarthmore chapter of the American Association of University Professors, with R. C. Brooks at the head. They informed me that they had considered my proposals, had approved of them individually and collectively, and wished to raise the question whether it was not time to begin. I was hardly ready myself, but they were, and accordingly we began at once. I appointed the appropriate committees and the academic year 1921-22 was spent in planning honors courses. From the beginning, as I have said, (we took Greats as our model and planned each honors course in co-operation between two or three related

[1] Frank Aydelotte, Inaugural Address: "Better Training for Our Best Minds," *Swarthmore College Bulletin*, XIX, 2, pp. 19-25. Twelfth month, 1921. Printed also in *School and Society*, November 5, 1921.

departments so as to give the student a program which would be clearly organized and focused upon a particular field, but not so narrowly specialized as would be the case were his work confined to a single department.)

We soon decided upon the (seminar method of teaching) as opposed to individual tutorials. From the start we decided that for (honors students the course and hour system should be abolished, that attendance at lectures and classes should be entirely voluntary, and that the honors degree should depend upon the student's success in a series of examinations, written and oral, conducted by external examiners. Our most important and most difficult task was to decide upon the content of these examinations.)

(The question as to what the student should be expected to know in order to qualify for a degree was a novel one, and the members of the faculty had no answers ready.) This is not the same as the question as to what ground should be covered by a series of lectures, or classes, or seminars. No one expects that a student will remember all that the professor says, or all that he himself reads, and on the other hand no one of us was quite prepared to predict what a good student would be able to do for himself by his own thinking about the material dealt with. (Our task was to prepare a kind of syllabus which could be given to the student at the beginning of the Junior year indicating the field he would be expected to master, and given at the end of the Senior year to the examiners whose task would be to determine how well he had mastered it.)

At the end of six months or so of constant work by various committees only two honors courses were sufficiently agreed upon to make it possible for students to begin the next year—English literature and the social sciences.) Accordingly, volunteers were called for in those two fields. A few students applied. Of these, eleven had made previous records good

enough to promise success in honors work and with them the
new plan went into effect in September, 1922.

The work, which was planned for two years, we subdivided
into four parts for the four semesters, and the part for each
semester into weeks, thus making a kind of program of reading and discussion for each seminar. The topic for a single
meeting was usually split up into four or five subtopics corresponding to the number of students, and each undergraduate
prepared a paper on one of these questions. In addition, all
the students concerned were held responsible for a common
background of reading which would enable them to discuss
intelligently each other's papers. For the first few years it was
our practice to have two members of the faculty attend each
seminar. Often there were more. Visitors who might contribute to the discussions were constantly brought in. For several
years I made it a point to visit every seminar in every subject
at least once a term.

We found undergraduates in general quite ready to assume
the additional responsibility for their own education placed
upon their shoulders by this plan. Inevitably they floundered at first, as honors students still do in their Junior
year, even though the college has had twenty years of experience with honors work. Members of the faculty floundered
also. In countless minor ways our methods had to be altered
from week to week and from term to term. Because the
numbers were small, changes could be made with a minimum
of confusion and by the time the enrollment in honors work
had increased to something like half the Juniors and Seniors
in college, we had gained a decade of useful experience.
During the early years we gave the students frequent opportunity to air their difficulties and grievances.

I well remember one such occasion. Dr. Abraham Flexner,
with his keen interest in every experiment that promised to

improve the quality of American undergraduate education, had become interested in what we were doing and had invited us to make an application to the General Education Board for financial assistance. A representative of the Board came to Swarthmore to inspect honors work at first hand. He came with only a few days notice, in the last week of term, when, instead of regular honors seminars, the entire group of honors students (at that time perhaps fifteen or twenty) were scheduled to meet together to exchange experiences, point out difficulties, and receive from the faculty explanation and encouragement.(It was my invariable rule never to alter any academic arrangement for the sake of a visitor, and I did not alter this meeting, though I feared it might not be a suitable one for such a visitor to attend.)

My worst fears were immediately realized. As soon as the meeting was opened one student after another began to hold forth on the defects of honors work. The requirements were vague. There were no definite assignments of so many pages to read, so many exercises to do, so many dates to learn. Instead they had to wrestle for themselves with a topic and a bibliography: they never knew how much would be expected of them, they did not know when they were through, they missed the definiteness of course work where specific tasks were assigned day by day, so that a man could know when he had finished his work and when he was free to play.

My heart sank and I thought I perceived that our visitor was embarrassed. But before I or any member of the faculty had time to reply to these objections, other undergraduates took up the discussion. They pointed out somewhat more sharply than would have been courteous on the part of a professor, that the whole theory of honors work was to place upon the student the responsibility for his own education, they intimated that possibly those who felt the need for such daily spoon-feeding were not themselves suited to the demands of independent study, they pointed out that undergraduates could hardly expect to develop initiative and independence unless they were given precisely the freedom which honors work offered. A lively discussion followed, which continued for two or three hours entirely between the students with hardly a word from any member of the faculty. When we left, our visitor pronounced the meeting the most impressive academic exercise he had ever attended and in due time the much needed financial assistance was forthcoming.

From the beginning there was great interest in other colleges and universities in the working of the plan at Swarthmore, and the college received many visitors who wished to inspect honors work. These visitors were of great benefit to us, particularly in the early years. We took pains to enable them to get what they were seeking. We opened all the seminars in the college to them freely and gave them as much opportunity as they wished to confer with students and with members of the faculty. When a visitor came it was my practice to call together at my house the members of the faculty in the field in which the visitor was interested to discuss honors work in all its aspects. Quite frequently in the early years a visitor would ask a question about our procedure or the theory on which it was based; some member of the faculty would reply, describing our practice; then another member would express a different opinion, whereupon the whole matter would be thrashed out, sometimes only after long debate. In this way we developed our methods during months and years of discussion and thus evolved not so much a transplantation of Oxford methods to Swarthmore as a system of our own based upon the same principles, but adapted to our conditions. I was interested in a remark by the

Master of Balliol made during a month spent at Swarthmore in 1930 that what struck him about our honors plan was not so much its resemblance to Oxford as its difference. (Nothing in the Oxford method of teaching, it seemed to us who knew both systems, quite took the place of the free discussion in our seminars.)

We were clear from the beginning at Swarthmore that honors degrees should depend solely upon the result of comprehensive examinations covering the Junior and Senior years, that no grades should be given on the student's work week by week or term by term, that if an honors student attended a course no record should be kept of his attendance, and that he should not be expected to take the term examination. We resolved that for two years we would devote ourselves to teaching him, leaving the result to be appraised by others after we of the faculty had done our best.

(Nevertheless we soon found that our selection of honors students was not infallible, and that some means had to be devised for eliminating those who proved to be unfitted for honors work.) Some students who had done well in courses were not able to make the same success of independent study. Others lost interest or decided upon some change in their program which would not fit into the honors plan. For these reasons it proved to be necessary to make a kind of continuous review of the progress of honors work term by term and to meet difficulties as they arose. This we found could readily be done by private informal discussion, without machinery or red tape. Members of the Swarthmore faculty are keenly interested in their students and are constantly discussing them. In an article about the college[2] Dorothy Canfield Fisher said that a dinner party at Swarthmore differed from dinner

[2] Dorothy Canfield Fisher, "Melting the Faculty Ice," *World's Work*, V. 58, pp. 52-56. May, 1929.

parties everywhere else in the nature of the conversation. A Swarthmore group would start off like any other, talking about the weather or travel in Europe or the most recent popular book, but sooner or later some professor would say something about one of his students and from then on no other subject had a chance. Since each honors student was working with at least two members of the faculty at a time and since he changed seminars each semester, there would always be several professors who had seen something of a given undergraduate in honors work, in addition to those who had taught him in his Freshman and Sophomore years. Cards and records were not needed; all the information necessary the members of the faculty carried in their heads. Decisions were taken on the basis of full discussion of each individual case, in the course of which differences of opinion might develop and heated arguments ensue. A student would be dropped from honors work only after the same kind of careful discussion that would be given to the question of terminating the appointment of an instructor.

Undergraduate initiative provided us after a few years with a valuable additional method of estimating the progress of honors students and of eliminating those who proved unfitted for individual work. A few years after honors work began I received a petition from the whole group of Junior honors students asking that they might be allowed to take the honors examinations in their subjects at the same time as the Seniors, answering only those questions for which their one year of honors work gave them material, and handing in their papers not to the external examiners, but to their own professors, for comment and criticism. The students felt that this experience would be a help to them when they faced the external examiners the following year and would be a valuable check-up on the progress they had made so far. We saw no reason why this petition should not be granted, and these trial Junior examinations have been ever since not exactly a requirement but certainly a fixed tradition which no one would think of violating. These trial examinations tell the Juniors a good deal about themselves and tell the faculty a good deal about the Juniors. No records are kept of the results. No student's standing is affected by them, except that in certain cases they may furnish to members of the faculty concrete evidence supporting the suggestion that a given individual should withdraw from honors work and go back to the ordinary course. Perhaps ten or fifteen per cent of those who begin honors work are eliminated in this way. Severity in this respect is really kindness and it safeguards the standard of honors work.

In the early days of the operation of the honors plan at Swarthmore the number of students involved was so small that discussion of individual cases might take place anywhere, in any one of our offices or houses, or wherever two or three members of the faculty might meet. After a few years someone proposed that the professors of each division should meet once a week for luncheon. The division of mathematics and the natural sciences chose Tuesday, the division of the humanities, Wednesday, and the social science division, Thursday. The deans, the comptroller, and I attended all three of these luncheons or as many of them as we could. The luncheon meetings thus started have been regularly held for more than fifteen years. There has never been any compulsion about attendance; professors pay for their own luncheons; those with engagements may have to "eat and run"; but interest has never flagged and the contribution which these meetings make to the unification of methods and attitudes is one of the great factors in the success of honors work. They furnish the equivalent of an Oxford College Meeting. Immediately after dessert, the chairman of the division makes necessary announcements and offers the opportunity to anyone present to bring up matters concerning honors work in the division. In the spring when Sophomore applicants for honors work are being considered, lists of names are handed around, each applicant is carefully discussed, and admitted or rejected by a vote of the three departments concerned, after hearing advice which may be freely offered by anyone present. At any time in the year Junior honors students whose work is unsatisfactory are discussed and their cases decided. Appeals which occasionally are sent in by students against the action of the faculty of the division are read at the following meeting and given such consideration as they seem to merit. These meetings make it possible to administer honors work by human rather than by mechanical methods. They have very much reduced the number and the length of our faculty meetings since a great deal of college business is discussed and disposed of week by week as need arises. These luncheons offer an ideal opportunity for the entertainment of visitors and for enabling them to meet those members of the faculty in whom they are most interested. They offer the opportunity, which most faculties do not have, for the free discussion of a problem by a responsible group without the necessity of voting or taking a decision. They offered to me as president the opportunity which I valued highly of making suggestions, obtaining an informal reaction to them, and of thus forming an opinion as to whether this or that change in our methods would be advisable.

When I first proposed external examiners for honors students, there was some hesitation on the part of the Swarthmore faculty before the idea was finally approved. One professor remarked, "This means that we are being examined as well as the students." That, of course, was exactly the point and after full discussion the faculty decided that there was no reason why that would not be a good thing. The plan was adopted and every year for twenty years it has become more firmly entrenched as a part of the Swarthmore system.

Not everyone is qualified to make a good examiner, but we have found no serious difficulty in securing suitable individuals. Our normal practice has been to ask an external examiner to serve for three years so that each year approximately one-third of the group would be new, but there are many exceptions due to the difficulty of arranging dates and schedules. We are proud of the quality of the men and women who serve the college in this capacity, and their names are printed each year in the Swarthmore catalogue. After an examiner is appointed he receives in due time outlines or syllabi which show the ground his examinees are supposed to have covered. On the basis of these outlines the examiner prepares his written questions and sends them to Swarthmore. The student has a period of about ten days or two weeks in which to write the seven or eight three-hour examinations which each will take. The blue books are mailed to the examiner as fast as they are written and when all are finished the examiners meet at Swarthmore for a period, usually of two days, during which they hold their oral examinations and consult together about the award of classes—honors, high honors, or highest honors as the case may be. The papers of a student whose work is not thought to be worthy of honors are returned to his department, the members of which then decide whether he should be awarded an ordinary degree at commencement, or whether he should be required to do further work during the summer and take additional tests in September. Because of the careful selection of honors students and the elimination during the Junior and Senior years of those who do not work well under the honors plan, failures are comparatively rare.

(The cost of external examiners, which was nominal at first, now amounts to about $2000 per year but the value of the contribution which these examiners have made to the development of honors work is out of all proportion to the cost. Every year after the examinations are finished the examiners will have many comments to make which members of the faculty find valuable, on the preparation of students, conduct of the work, the reason for the inclusion of one topic or the exclusion of another, or on the relative emphasis given to various phases of the subject. These comments are made informally, although a particularly interesting one may be discussed at divisional luncheons the next fall or indeed quoted for years afterwards.

Twenty years of honors work at Swarthmore have produced extraordinary changes in the atmosphere of the college. Of all the changes produced the most intangible and most important is the improvement in morale of students and members of the faculty alike. This seems to me fully as important from the point of view of building character as for its intellectual value. The best index of character is the sincerity and honesty and faithfulness with which an individual does his work. If an educational institution can be induced to put first things first, to subordinate everything else to its main business of education and scholarship, it will be sincere in a way that it cannot be if its principal pride is in its athletic teams or in some other irrelevant activity. That sincerity will make it a better place in which young people can live and grow.

American students are deeply in earnest about their education. They are quick to acquire that sense of proportion which will cause them to put work first and play second.

Nor will their play be any less whole-hearted and delightful on that account. During recent years at Swarthmore the system of athletics has been thoroughly reorganized in order to secure wider participation in sports by members of the student body. This was not done by the tame system of intramural athletics. Instead the number of teams in each sport was increased; in the place of one team in each sport we organized from two to four, each playing a schedule of games against outside opponents. The result is that now nearly seventy percent of the men represent the college in contests with other institutions. For most of these games there are no spectators and no cheering. The standard of play is not so high as it would be if all the energy of the college were devoted to the development of one varsity team. But these contests are good fun for all concerned; all the essential values of athletics are preserved with none of the evils. So sensible and delightful a plan for athletic sports has been possible and successful partly because the character of the academic work of the college has been such as to lead students to put athletics in their place and not make them the main business of college life.

Something of the same kind has happened in the case of social activities. The complaint that in American academic life the side-shows seem to the students more important than the main performance may be due to the fact that the main performance has too often not been sufficiently difficult and adventurous to demand the best effort from the best. When that is corrected, when the academic program demands the utmost effort of the ablest students, all the other activities of college life fall into their rightful place. No negative regulation is necessary. Point systems and other devices for limiting the participation of students in extra-curricular activities are no longer needed. The best students, who set the pace and start the fashions, will make the right choices and the atmosphere of the college will change from that of a country club to that of an educational institution.[3]

[3] For fuller details on this point see *An Adventure in Education*, by the Swarthmore College Faculty, Macmillan, 1941, Chapters X and XII. (The Swarthmore College Book Store, Swarthmore, Pa., has for sale all the available supply of this volume.) This book presents the fullest and most up-to-date account of honors work at Swarthmore considered in its relationship to all parts of the educational program of the College. An earlier account, still useful and suggestive, is Robert C. Brooks' *Reading for Honors at Swarthmore*, Oxford University Press, 1927. A briefer essay, Frank Aydelotte, "Honors Courses at Swarthmore," is printed as a chapter in *Five College Plans*, Columbia University Press, 1931.

CHAPTER FIVE

FIRST STEPS: HONORS WORK AS AN EXTRA

THERE are about two hundred colleges and universities in the list approved by the Association of American Universities. In nearly three-quarters of them attempts are being made to provide special facilities for the best and most ambitious students, freeing them from the regimentation of average standards and giving them opportunities to go forward at a faster pace. I propose in this and the three following chapters to describe and discuss some of these plans which are now in operation.

These programs fall naturally into three groups: (1) those in which honors work is an extra activity over and above the ordinary requirements for graduation, (2) those in which honors work is allowed to replace a certain number of courses, usually one or two courses in the Junior and Senior years, and (3) those in which honors work replaces entirely the regular curriculum during the two upper years. The first type is discussed at the end of this chapter and I have devoted a separate chapter to each of the other two. In various state universities honors work follows all three of the plans indicated and in addition, in a few of them, an attempt is made to provide special treatment for those students who for various reasons fall below the average standard. A separate chapter is devoted to these interesting innovations.

The way in which information was obtained about the working of these various honors plans is explained in the Preface. About one hundred and thirty colleges and universities have been visited and studied by Swarthmore professors. The reports on these visits give a most heartening impression of the present state of American higher education. It is true that in many places only the merest beginning has been made, and in very few are the programs sufficiently thoroughgoing to approach an adequate solution of the problem. (Almost everywhere opposition has been encountered from members of the faculty, from students, from alumni, and from trustees. This opposition has proved to be strongest in some of the best places where the quality of student body and faculty, the generosity of the endowments, and the excellence of the equipment might have made an ambitious plan of honors work most successful, while the greatest enthusiasm is sometimes found in places which lack all these advantages.) Nevertheless, in most of the best colleges and universities a beginning has been made, the first step has been taken, and any change is likely to be in a forward direction. Instances can be found where radical plans have been hastily adopted before they were generally understood either by faculty or students, tried for a few years, and then abandoned. But such places are rare; the overwhelming number have chosen to begin slowly, meet opposition step by step, solve problems as they arise, and thus lay the foundation for solid growth.

This book is a record of solid achievement already accomplished, but perhaps the most gratifying feature of the situation today is the fact that the need for better facilities for our best students is being more and more keenly realized, that the movement to provide such facilities is daily gathering momentum, and that after the war significant further progress may be expected.

Before embarking on the description of the various plans which form the subject matter of this and the three following chapters, it seems important in the interests of completeness to notice (certain programs foreshadowing the methods of honors work which have been followed in various American colleges and universities since the beginning of the last quarter of the nineteenth century) It is, furthermore, worth noting that the freer methods of study which are usual under honors plans have had their effect in producing in a few institutions more flexible programs of study applied to all students and not restricted to the best and most ambitious. It is an easy transition from these plans to those in which honors work is an extra, the description of which forms the final portion of this chapter.

(While honors work) in the sense in which the term is here used, has been developed only during the last twenty-five years,) tentative steps in that direction had been taken in various places long before. At Wesleyan, honors at commencement are said to have been given for a thesis and an approved arrangement of courses since 1873. In 1883 there was inaugurated at Michigan the so-called University System which excused abler students from the regular requirements and allowed them to follow a freer and more specialized program of studies, to be tested by a searching examination at the end of the Senior year. The plan operated successfully for eight years and was carried in the catalogue down to 1900. While there was no provision for independent tutorial work, the plan did offer special facilities for abler students, brought them into closer contact with members of the faculty, and required them to pass examinations which were more severe than those taken by the rank and file. Among the small group of students who were graduated under this plan an unusually large proportion rose to distinction and they uniformly looked back upon the opportunity offered at Michigan with the greatest enthusiasm.[1]

The award of honors on the basis of a thesis still in vogue at the University of Vermont dates from 1888; the preceptorial system at Princeton was established in 1905; the program of study for honors based upon the classics of the western world, adopted at Columbia in 1920, replaced an older plan of honors work which had existed for more than a decade before. The University of Missouri adopted a plan of reading for honors in 1912 but abandoned it in 1926 (to resume it again in recent years) and at about the same time the University of Washington under the leadership of Dean Padelford adopted regulations allowing students chosen as Senior Scholars to do the work of the Senior year entirely by independent study instead of taking courses. This plan, because of opposition from conservative members of the faculty, was allowed to continue for only a few years.

In 1914, at Harvard, general examinations and the tutorial system were established in the division of history and political science, and in 1916 plans for honors work substantially the same as those in vogue at present were begun at Lafayette College and at Rice Institute. Honors work was begun at Smith in 1921 and in Swarthmore in 1922. In 1925 a conference on the subject was held at the State University of Iowa presided over by Dr. Vernon Kellogg of the National Research Council. Among the speakers who strongly advocated the new methods were Dean Effinger of Michigan, Dean Johnston of Minnesota, Dean Wilkins then of Chicago, and Dean Seashore of the University of Iowa. The tenor of the

[1] For a fuller account of this interesting program see Frank Aydelotte, "The University System at Michigan," *Michigan Alumnus*, XLII, 23, pp. 228-233, June 27, 1936.

addresses, as summarized by Miss Gladys Palmer in an article in *School and Society* for June 20, 1925, shows that the idea was then the subject of serious consideration and active discussion in various institutions in the Middle West. Since 1925 developments have been rapid. Plans have been widely adopted and have been made the subject of voluminous discussion in educational periodicals.

(So strong is the impulse throughout the country to break the tyranny of the rigid course and hour system that it affects many institutions which have so far been unwilling to provide any special facilities for their better students.) In these places freer programs involving more scope for individual initiative are provided for all. Bowdoin College is one example. No separation is made between the best students and the average; for graduation every student has since 1921 been required to take a comprehensive examination in his major field. Those students who do particularly well in this examination, or who have done work of a high grade in preparing for it in essays, theses, or reports, are recommended by the department for honors. In some departments there are special conferences arranged for the honors men. In other departments everything depends upon the examination. Johns Hopkins is another example. This is no formal honors plan but much of the work is individual and is done in the spirit of an honors college.

From 1931 to 1934 Colgate maintained a system of honors work providing a freer and more severe program for the abler students. In 1934 this plan was abandoned and a method of individual teaching was worked out for all students, including preceptorials for Freshmen, tutorials for Sophomores, and seminars for upperclass students. This individual work occupies one hour per week for Freshmen and Sophomores and takes one-fifth of the student's time in the Junior and Senior years. There is a comprehensive examination in the major subject which all must pass for graduation.

At the University of Buffalo all of the upper-college work is on a tutorial basis. No student is admitted to the Junior year unless his standing is sufficiently high and his promise great enough to induce the department in which he wishes to concentrate to accept him as a tutorial student. Degrees are awarded on the basis of comprehensive examinations, both written and oral. It has been said that the policy of the Senior College section of the University of Buffalo is to admit only students of honors caliber. The examinations, however, are so searching that only a fraction of those who take them are awarded honors at commencement.

The plan at Wabash is somewhat similar in that every student is theoretically a candidate for honors. Since 1932 no one has been graduated from Wabash except after passing comprehensive examinations in one of four divisions. On the basis of their performance in these examinations men are awarded first, second, or third honors, or merely a pass. Students must select courses to prepare themselves for their comprehensives and all are given special reading courses leading to them in the Senior year. While the college still keeps up the standard requirement of a hundred and twenty hours of credit for graduation, emphasis for honors is entirely upon general grasp of a subject and success in comprehensive examinations. Both students and faculty are keenly interested in the plan and its effect is said to have been to improve greatly the work which undergraduates do, particularly in the Junior and Senior years.

While it is not a program of honors work in the sense in which that term is used in this volume, the Chicago College plan is an impressive experiment in the application of freer methods to all students. The College of the University of Chicago differs in several important ways from the conventional liberal arts college. Its program begins two years earlier than that of other colleges, permitting students to enter after two years of high school instead of four. Its course of study consists of an integrated system of courses covering the principal fields of knowledge rather than an assortment of courses chosen by the student himself. It expects students to complete the work of the College at seventeen or eighteen when he would conventionally be finishing his sophomore year, and then to proceed with specialized (divisional) or professional work. It measures the achievements of students and determines their eligibility for the Bachelor's degree by comprehensive examinations. Course credits and course marks that count toward the attainment of a degree have been abolished, and the student may take the comprehensive examinations whenever he feels that he is ready. The program gives students considerable freedom with respect to class attendance and class work. In some of the courses offered in preparation for comprehensive examinations superior students are not held back to the pace of the average; instead special sections are arranged which go faster and further than the ordinary classes, while "trailer" sections meet the needs of those who find it difficult to maintain the average pace.

The purpose of the College of the University of Chicago is to give the student a broad general education. The core of the curriculum consists of general courses in the biological sciences, the humanities, the physical sciences, and the social sciences. As students acquire information and learn to think for themselves, they should develop the ability to communicate their knowledge. The student, therefore, normally takes a three-year course in writing. In the last year of the College he takes a course in principles and methods designed to assist him to integrate properly the studies he has pursued. The College curriculum includes work in mathematics and foreign languages for students who enter with deficiencies in these subjects, or who desire to increase their mastery of them, or who need such work in preparation for later specialized or professional training. The most significant aspects of the Chicago plan from the point of view of this study are that it provides (1) a common intellectual background for all students and (2) variation in standard of work and rapidity of progress in accordance with individual ability. The fundamental difference between the Chicago plan and honors work as described in this volume is that the flexibility of the Chicago method applies to the rapidity and thoroughness with which students of different levels of ability prepare for comprehensive examinations, which are the same for all. The examinations set at the University of Chicago are, however, deliberately framed so that no student can answer all questions perfectly. In this way they attempt to test the capacity of the most brilliant student and at the same time reflect any degree of achievement on the part of the poorest.

These institutions illustrate trends which will probably affect all undergraduate work sooner or later. We may expect that higher standards and freer, less rigid methods of instruction will gradually permeate our whole academic system. Such methods, however, which demand initiative and intellectual curiosity, may be expected to work best with students who possess those qualities in a high degree and it is noteworthy that, in places where freer methods of study are open to all, the reports indicate that these methods are most popular with the best students. It is true that the spoon-feeding characteristic of the course and hour system underestimates the ability of even the average student, and that undergraduates of modest capacity have much to gain by freer methods which lay more responsibility on their shoulders and call for greater independence in their work. It is all to the good that individual instruction for all students in tutorial conferences or small seminars is becoming more and more common and that comprehensive examinations for the A.B. degree are now held in the majority of the approved colleges and universities of the country.

Another device, now being tried out at a few places, among them Harvard, Yale, and Princeton, is the reading period—an interval of two or three weeks at the end of each semester when no classes or lectures are held and when students have the opportunity for solid reading and study for which their regular schedule left insufficient time. The reading period has proved popular with members of the faculty as affording the opportunity for uninterrupted research. It is said to be well used by the best students, but to mean less for the less ambitious. Even for the best students it may be questioned whether a less rigid program of classes and lectures might not be better, extending, so to speak, the reading period throughout the year.

As I indicated at the beginning of this chapter, fully organized plans for honors work which are now in operation in about a hundred and thirty colleges and universities fall naturally, in spite of many differences of detail, into three main groups: (1) those in which honors work is an extra; (2) those in which honors work replaces one or more of the regular courses; (3) those in which honors work entirely replaces the ordinary academic program. In the paragraphs following I give some examples of honors work of the first type and have devoted Chapters VI and VII to the second and third.

In those institutions where no modification of the regular course requirements is made, students (for the most part

Seniors) who show unusual interest and aptitude in their studies may be allowed to undertake honors work as an extra over and above course requirements. The extra reading or laboratory work is individually supervised by a member of the faculty, either in regularly scheduled tutorial conferences or in irregular and casual meetings as the case may be. Usually the results of the work are embodied in a thesis and sometimes the student is given an examination, either written or oral, over the extra work he has done. The scope of this examination may be widened so as to make it a comprehensive test of all his work in his major department, or, when such a comprehensive examination is required of all students, the honors examination may constitute an addition to it. A good thesis or meritorious showing in this special examination may be rewarded by some kind of honors on commencement day, though in some cases the work is left to be its own reward.

In plans of this type there is no relaxation of the course requirements for the A.B. degree, and usually no allowance is made in the teaching schedule of the professors concerned for the time spent in individual supervision of this independent work. The whole thing is an extra task for teachers and students. The fact that under these circumstances independent work should still be undertaken by considerable numbers of students offers striking testimony to the vitality of the plan, to the intellectual interests of American college students, and to the desire of American college professors to do their work well.

Honors work at Wooster must be done as an addition to whatever program the student is following. An undergraduate who has made a good enough record in the first two years and who elects, on his own initiative, to do so, may, before the end of his Sophomore year, make application to work for honors. He selects an adviser in the department in which the honors work will be done, and that adviser directs his studies. Methods of instruction vary in different departments and include both tutorial conferences and seminars. A thesis is required, as well as both an oral and a written examination, one of which is comprehensive. In spite of indifference on the part of some members of the faculty (the supervision of honors work is an extra for the faculty, and the faculty-student ratio is 1:15) about ten per cent of each Senior class take their degrees with honors. This percentage is the more remarkable because of the fact that the standard of quality of honors work is kept extremely high.

The so-called departmental honors plan at Emory University is of a similar character. Highly qualified students may be invited by their departments to undertake a program of independent study for honors, this work to be done in addition to the regular requirements for graduation. A careful program is made out for each candidate by his department or by him in consultation with his professors, and this program must receive the approval of the dean and the honors committee of the faculty. Each student submits to a special oral examination covering the work he has done for honors, conducted by a committee consisting of representatives of his own and of related departments, including a member of the honors committee. The majority of the best students participate in the plan and from three to ten per cent of the members of each Senior class receive their degrees with honors.

Honors work at Agnes Scott College is similar to that at Emory University though students undertaking it are allowed to reduce their course work from fifteen hours to thirteen and arrangements are made for tutorial supervision. This tutorial work is an extra burden for members of the faculty concerned. The rules for honors examinations at Agnes Scott provide for the use of one external examiner as a member of each committee. Both of these plans are carefully administered and one may expect that as their success is more fully demonstrated they will be developed and that fuller allowance will be made for honors work in the time both of students and of members of the faculty.

At Dickinson honors work consists of the preparation of a thesis and the undergoing of an examination on it, all this over and above the regular course requirements for the A.B. degree. It has been observed that some students avoid honors work because it inevitably lessens the amount of time they can spend on their regular courses and thus diminishes their chances of qualifying for Phi Beta Kappa.

The honors plan at Middlebury, which is similar, was started in 1917 and took its present form in 1922. At Middlebury honors work consists of a certain amount of independent study and research tested by examination. This individual study may culminate in a thesis, and it frequently does, but a thesis is not necessarily required. Honors work is an extra over and above the regular course requirements for the A.B. degree. Here also some students avoid honors work because as an additional load it inevitably lessens the amount of time they can spend on their regular courses. Plans of a similar character, in that the work involved is an extra both for students and members of the faculty, are being followed at Lafayette, at Mt. Union, and at Southern Methodist University. Viewed as experimental beginnings they are admirable and offer eloquent testimony to the intellectual interests of the students and members of the faculty concerned, but all experience indicates that it will be difficult in the long run to keep up interest unless the work becomes eventually an integral part of the program and is not left merely as an extra.

The drawback to such plans as these is, of course, the element of time. Both professors and students are carrying full schedules of regular work.) Only the keenest and most energetic minds will be able to carry on independent work in hours supposed to be devoted to leisure, and the best will be able to accomplish only a fraction of what they could do with more freedom. It is not surprising that where independent work is entirely an extra, only a small proportion of students and faculty have the courage and the interest to undertake it. The typical college or university which attempts to provide special facilities for a larger group of its abler students, as the next chapter shows, takes account to some extent of these objections.

CHAPTER SIX

PART-TIME HONORS PLANS

UNDER the typical American honors plan, superior students, usually those with an average of B or better, are allowed to substitute in the Junior and Senior years a so-called honors course for one of the five courses usually carried. The honors course is normally in the major subject. It consists of independent reading or laboratory work, and is supervised either by individual tutorial conferences or in small honors seminars. It is tested as a rule both by a thesis and by a comprehensive examination set by members of the department. In many cases these examinations are oral, sometimes both oral and written. The nature of the independent work may vary from a broad course of reading of the survey type to a piece of intensive research in which the student endeavors to find out something not known before, but it consists usually of more intensive study of some phase of the work regularly offered by the department. Honors are awarded on commencement day, partly on the basis of the showing made by the student in his independent work, partly on the average of his grades throughout his course. Often the honors course is graded like any other and the grade given for it counted in his general average. This is unfortunate. Since the independent honors course is likely to be harder and more severely tested than the regular courses in the curriculum, the student who does honors work may, by doing so, lessen his chances of receiving commencement honors or of being elected to Phi Beta Kappa.) This fact does not escape the students, and the number of undergraduates who enroll for work of this type is smaller on that account.

Under the typical arrangements which I have described the supervision of independent work is sometimes counted as a part of the professor's regular teaching schedule, sometimes imposed upon him as an extra burden. (Where individual tutorial work or honors seminars are counted as a regular part of a professor's duties, the expense of instruction for the college or university is, of course, somewhat increased. The increase could in many cases be wholly or partially met by curtailing the number of small advanced specialized courses offered by departments. The number and variety of such courses represent a great extravagance in American higher education.) A few small colleges are courageously limiting the number of courses offered as a means of finding faculty time for honors work, and it may well be that the soundness of instruction in such an institution may in the future be partly judged by the thinness of its catalogue. For the most part, however, this method of economy has not been adopted, and in too many places whatever additional expense honors work may involve is borne by the faculty in the form of extra hours of teaching.

Honors work at Brown University is a conservative example of the part-time plan. Qualified students undertake honors study in their major fields, departmental or inter-departmental, during their Junior and Senior years. Honors work varies greatly from field to field to suit the nature of the subject studied. One aim is to unify and deepen the student's grasp of the whole field of his major; another is to develop his intellectual initiative and independence through special study or research of particular interest to him. Instruction may be by individual tutorials or in seminars or in special courses limited to honors students. In almost every case a Senior thesis is required. There is a comprehensive examination, the standard of which is severe. Student interest is keen; in the three years 1940-42 approximately fifteen per cent of the Seniors received their degrees with honors. The plan is a good illustration of the excellent work which may be done with a minimum of interference with the ordinary academic program.

Honors work at Bryn Mawr may replace a total of one and a half courses in the Junior and Senior years. It consists of work of a more advanced character than that done in regular courses; it is done under tutorial supervision; one or two long papers or reports are required, and the standard of the comprehensive examinations taken by all students for the degree is higher for candidates for honors. The regulations allow the employment of outside examiners, but up to the date of inspection they had never been used. Student interest is keen, about one-quarter of the Senior class being enrolled as candidates for honors.

At Wellesley candidates for honors in a special field may substitute a course of independent directed study for one of the regular courses in the Senior year and in connection with it prepare a thesis. The work often extends beyond the confines of one subject and the members of the student's advisory committee may be drawn from as many as three departments. Although students are permitted to begin in the Junior year, this is rarely done. The work is tested by a comprehensive oral examination.

A second plan for departmental honors has been recently inaugurated at Wellesley designed to enable outstanding students to enrich the work of the major field by engaging in a program of supplementary directed study during the Senior year. A candidate for departmental honors carries the full Senior program of courses and in addition engages in independent work under the guidance of some member of the faculty in her major department. Supplementary work may be used to fill gaps in the major field, to deepen knowledge of some particular period or topic, or to develop a connection with some related field. The work is tested by a general examination plus an oral at the end of the Senior year.

Grinnell also offers honors work in the major subject which is usually a definite part of the course of study. The amount of credit varies. In the English department, half of the time of the Senior year is devoted to the honors course, sixteen hours for the year. This work is concluded by a thesis and an oral examination. This is extra for the instructor but it is a part of the student's regular load.

Goucher has abandoned the hour-credit system and requires, in addition to course examinations, a series of tests at the end of the second year for admission to the Junior class and a formal comprehensive examination in the major subject for the A.B. degree. The college requires attendance of all students at so-called integration seminars, the purpose of which is to supplement work in courses and thus better prepare them for the comprehensive examinations. Over and above this program there is an independent study plan open to the best students leading to special honors at graduation. This may occupy one-third of the student's time for two of the three terms of the Senior year. Independent study consists of directed research leading to a thesis. The merit of the thesis is appraised by members of the faculty who have nothing to do with the instruction of the writer and their verdict determines whether the candidate will or will not receive honors at graduation.

On the average, nine per cent of graduates of Goucher

College receive special honors. In 1939 sixty-four per cent of those receiving special honors were elected to Phi Beta Kappa and of the whole group receiving Phi Beta Kappa forty-eight per cent were also granted honors. Both instructors and students are reported to be enthusiastic over the working of the plan.

At Kenyon College honors students are selected on the basis of the excellence of their work in the first two years and a student must be accepted both by his department and by the division in which he proposes to do honors work. Under regulations adopted in 1942, the nature of the honors work now depends entirely upon departmental rules with the approval of the division. Honors candidates are examined by one outside examiner who sets and grades the written examination and who conducts the oral. Experience with honors work has led the Kenyon faculty to reorganize the curriculum for all students according to a plan which allows them to concentrate on fewer subjects at a time.

Honors work was conducted at Oberlin from 1920 to 1930 as an extra over and above regular course requirements. In 1930 the plan was changed so as to allow honors work to replace at least one course during the Junior and Senior years. For admission to honors work a student must have an average of B plus in his major subject and B in all other work. Instruction may be in special honors courses, in seminars, or by individual direction of independent study. Honors work is tested by a preliminary examination at the end of the Junior year and, at the close of the Senior year, by comprehensive examinations both written and oral. The plan is carefully administered and deserves more students than usually enroll under it. The number of honors graduates has never been more than ten per cent of the Senior class, often fewer. Reasons given for the lack of wider popularity of the plan are the high quality of the ordinary work of the college, and the number of serious and worth-while extra-curricular activities in music and public affairs. Probably an additional reason is that in many instances the supervision of honors work is an extra for members of the faculty who are already teaching a heavy schedule of large classes. Belief in the plan, however, is so strong among both professors and students who do participate in it that it seems likely to be extended.

Degrees with distinction at Wesleyan are awarded upon the successful completion of a program which includes certain special courses in the major department and outside fields, plus a tutorial course which involves independent study or laboratory work and sometimes a thesis, plus success in a comprehensive examination. The tutorial work replaces one out of ten courses required in the last two years. Candidates for degrees with distinction (about one-half of the Senior class and one-third of the Juniors) are admitted to membership in the Honors College which was opened in 1937 in a historic mansion presented to the college by Thomas M. Russell, Jr. Russell House is used as a center for honors work and for informal gatherings of the students and faculty of the Honors College. The prestige of membership and the interest of the general activities of the Honors College are doubtless partly responsible for the large number of candidates for degrees with distinction. Wesleyan has made generous provision for honors teaching, and interest is at a high level, both among students and members of the faculty who have participated in honors work.

At Williams College honors work likewise may replace not more than one course in each of the Junior and Senior years. An undergraduate who has made a good enough record in the first two years is notified in the middle of the Sophomore year that he is eligible to choose work leading to the degree with honors. The standard required is in general B. If he accepts he enrolls in an honors course in his major subject which provides opportunity for independent work with individual instruction. Usually a thesis is required in the Senior year and at the end of the year a special honors examination. About twenty per cent of the Seniors take their degrees with honors. Members of the faculty believe that honors work has increased the number of Williams graduates who go on to postgraduate training and that it has prepared them better for success in graduate school. The experience of Williams well illustrates the tonic effect which even a limited plan of honors work sincerely administered may have upon a college.

Park College has maintained since 1927 an honors program to which selected students may give about one-third of their time in the Junior and two-thirds in the Senior year. Honors work is confined to the major subject. It is tested by a thesis and by comprehensive examinations, the oral part of which is given by external examiners. More than half of those who take the degree with honors enter graduate and professional schools. It is reported that the establishment of honors work at the University of Kansas was stimulated by the experiences of Kansas professors who had acted as external examiners at Park College.

Honors work at the College of the City of New York varies in different divisions but in all it is essentially an assignment of research projects, tested by a thesis and in some instances by a comprehensive examination. In some cases these theses are narrowly specialized, and are of such quality that some of them are published. Seminars are held for the discussion of research problems and the student's work is supervised by a tutor. The work varies in character between departments. In the social science division a serious effort has been made to transcend departmental lines in the honors work. While the special research project remains under departmental supervision, candidates for honors also are required to take a comprehensive examination testing their general grasp of the entire field and their understanding of the interrelations of the various social sciences. A reading list has been prepared for this purpose and monthly meetings are held at which the topics discussed are of general interest, drawn from the reading list and not from the individual research projects. The success of the plan illustrates the fact too often not realized that able undergraduates can do research of real value, though many professors, including some at C.C.N.Y., would question whether at this stage of his development it would not be better for an undergraduate to use independent work as a means of laying a solid foundation by the mastery of the elements of his subject. In some departments at C.C.N.Y. the work conforms to this purpose. There are about 100 honors students in the institution and the results obtained are impressive.

At Hunter College a somewhat similar program is followed. Commissioner Herlands of the Department of Investigation of New York City has a small group of picked students from Hunter working at special research problems in economics and sociology. The student spends twelve hours a week and the work counts as one course. The study is well supervised and faculty time so used is deducted from regular teaching schedules. The work is real, stimulating, and productive of tangible results. Both faculty and students are enthusiastic about it.

Under regulations promulgated by the Faculty Council of Hunter College in the spring of 1943 a plan of honors work has been authorized for all departments. For admission to this work a B average in the first two years is required. Each student so admitted is allowed to work out with her adviser an honors program of thirty credits of work in her major or in related departments, of which twelve credits are completed in the Junior and eighteen in the Senior year. These thirty credits may be divided between course work and guided reading in any way approved by the adviser, with the proviso that at least three credits in the Senior year shall be devoted to tutorial study. The work is tested both by comprehensive examination and by a thesis. It is possible that the "Herlands work" described above may eventually be included under the same regulations.

Plans of this type of equal interest are in operation at Amherst, Bates, Beloit, Boston University, Clark, Haverford, Howard College, Lehigh, Northwestern, Sweet Briar, Wilson, and many other colleges. They differ from one another in details, but all follow the common American custom of combining honors work with regular courses.

Honors work at Duke University approaches the full-time plans described in the next chapter. High-ranking students follow a special honors program which supersedes the regular one during the last two years. They do part of their work, however, in regular classes, in which they are held for the ordinary course examinations, and only part in special seminars or by independent reading. The plan is strictly departmentalized, and requirements vary from one department to another. Degrees are awarded on the basis of a comprehensive written examination plus an oral set by professors who have not taught the candidates. Although numbers have hitherto been small the students concerned are reported to be enthusiastic about the opportunity thus offered for independent work.

The programs which have just been described are typical of those in force in the majority of the American colleges and universities which offer special facilities for their best students. The course and hour system is partially, but not wholly, replaced by independent work. Honors work is confined to the major department and outside his major the student takes regular courses.

The typical procedure allowing one honors or independent study course to replace an ordinary course during the Junior and Senior years is a good beginning and admirable as far as it goes. For the most part students and faculty are enthusiastic about it wherever it is in force. It has, however, one great drawback, namely, lack of time for concentration upon independent work. Sometimes this difficulty is partially met by allowing independent study to replace as many as two courses, rarely more. This is better, but still the student is pulled in two directions at once. He is free for part of his time but not for all. He cannot organize his work entirely. Members of faculties who are on leave for part time for independent work, or who try to combine research with a light teaching schedule know only too well how seriously a few fixed engagements interfere with the prosecution of any large-scale undertaking. It is the same with undergraduates. The combination of some regular course work with a program of independent study is not impossible, but it is difficult. Perhaps the difficulties offer a discipline useful in its way, but a larger measure of freedom and concentration will certainly produce more tangible results.

Nevertheless, for plans organized on a departmental basis, freedom from two courses is about as far as faculties feel themselves justified in going. The devotion of nearly half the student's time to one department through the Junior and Senior years involves as great a degree of specialization as most faculties think advisable for undergraduates. In this I believe they are right and any plan of independent study involving the whole of the student's time in the last two years should be arranged by a combination of two or more departments.)

The plans for honors work and independent study at Columbia, Harvard, and Stanford, while resembling in general the programs described above, contain significant individual features. Each institution offers unusual opportunities to superior students and each makes its own unique contribution to the common fund of American experience in dealing with this problem.

Honors work at Columbia has had a long and interesting history. The faculty has experimented both with plans designed to broaden the interests and culture of the students by the study of great masterpieces of various periods and subjects, and with other plans designed to give the student a deeper mastery of the material of a single limited field. At present both types of work are offered to superior students; neither has any necessary connection with honors at graduation.

Columbia College developed about 1920 under the leadership of Professor John Erskine an honors plan which was essentially a Junior and Senior reading course in great books from Homer to Freud. On this work the student spent about one-quarter of his time and in addition was supposed to undertake a special honors program in a department by doing independent work in a single subject. This whole plan was abandoned in 1928 but the first part of it was revived in 1932 as a *colloquium* on important books—a two-hour reading course open to upperclassmen who had demonstrated their fitness during the first two years. The reading follows the bibliography of the old general honors course, now reprinted by the American Library Association under the title *Classics of the Western World*. Selections of material are made on the basis of the interests of the professors and students in any particular group. Undergraduates enter the course by invitation; admission, which is carefully guarded, is based upon general character and intellectual interests, determined in a personal interview, as well as upon course grades. Emphasis is placed upon the importance of the books read, as documents in the history of Western culture, rather than upon scholarly minutiae. The *colloquia* are conducted under able leadership and the great resources of the Columbia faculty are used for the provision of background lectures. The round-table discussions which ensue are lively and interesting and the members of a *colloquium* acquire through the two-year period an intellectual intimacy with each other and with the professor in charge which adds greatly to the value of the experience.[1]

In addition to the *colloquia*, Columbia now offers to qualified Juniors and Seniors honors work which may be (1) intensive work in a single department, (2) concentration in a field embracing two or more related departments, or (3) studies in a wider range of interests than those represented by a single department or a single division. The method of work is flexible and may consist of an individual program of reading; independent work in a laboratory; a seminar, or a read-

---

[1] The little pamphlet *Classics of the Western World* is one of the significant documents in the history of higher education in this country. Aside from its use at Columbia, the point of view which it represents has influenced the programs of the University of Chicago and St. John's College at Annapolis. An introductory honors course of the same character was proposed to the President of the University of Virginia by a committee in 1935, but was never acted upon by the faculty. It was intended to provide during the first two years, by the use of a selected list of the greatest classics from Greek times down to the present, a broad liberal education for a small group of the best students. These students would then be expected during their last two years to follow the honors program now in use at Virginia, with some modifications and improvements regarded by the committee as desirable.

ing course; certain chosen lecture courses; or any combination of these. Each student makes his own plan of study in conference with the appropriate committee, which committee also supervises his examinations and his thesis.

In addition to the two plans of honors work indicated, certain departments offer to students of exceptional ability the opportunity to substitute for regular courses independent reading courses, undergraduate seminars, and sometimes the opportunity to take postgraduate courses. Work of this character is offered in many departments and has been most fully developed in economics.

Special facilities for the best students at Harvard and Radcliffe are an outgrowth of certain innovations made during the last thirty years which were designed in the first place to improve the work of the entire student body. These innovations include: (1) the rules for concentration and distribution introduced about 1910, which ended the absolutely free operation of the elective system; (2) the reading period introduced in 1927 providing the opportunity for independent work for all students; (3) general examinations for the A.B. degree, introduced in 1914, which have had the effect of causing students to concentrate their work in a major field to a far greater extent than had been the practice previously; and (4) the tutorial system, which was an outgrowth of the general examination and the need of providing some orderly method of preparing for it.

These opportunities are open to all students without distinction as to ability. For some years, tutorial instruction at Harvard was divided into two plans: Plan A for the abler students, and Plan B for those of average ability. Students chosen for Plan A met their professors more frequently, and while candidacy for honors was not theoretically limited to

Plan A, in practice only men who qualified for this plan had the ambition to compete. The faculty has recently approved a regulation giving course credit for tutorial work for a maximum of two courses out of a total of sixteen. This rule, which goes into effect with the class of 1945, abolishes the old distinction between Plans A and B.

Honors at Harvard are awarded on the basis of general examinations offered now in twenty-seven fields of concentration, plus an honors thesis and the student's record in courses. A great deal of weight is given to the thesis, especially in the awarding of degrees *magna cum laude* and *summa cum laude*. Awards are made on the basis of the recommendation of the division, approved by the faculty. The faculty scrutinizes individually the recommendations for the degree *summa cum laude*, and that degree can only be voted by the faculty as a whole.

The authorities at Harvard emphasize the fact that the function of the tutor is not to cram or coach the student but rather to guide him in some form of individual work adjusted to his special interests and aptitudes. The arrangement which allows course credit for tutorial work gives the students more time for individual work under the tutor's direction.

In 1925 Stanford University introduced a university independent study plan designed to offer to abler students in the upper division the opportunity of spending from one-third to one-half of the time of the two upper years in guided independent work, replacing courses and terminating in comprehensive oral examinations. The reading was done according to individual plans supplied by the students and their advisers and approved by the University committee. The reading might or might not cut across departmental lines.

The success of this work led to the provision six years later, in 1931, of facilities for independent study in connection with certain important Freshman and Sophomore courses, in English, economics, history, political science, psychology, and sociology. As a further extension of the same principle, departments were encouraged in 1934 to carry on individual directed reading within departments in the Junior year. It was hoped that independent study in lower-division courses and directed independent reading within departments would accustom students to this method of work and increase their interest in more comprehensive work under the university plan in their Junior and Senior years.

This hope has been up to date only partially fulfilled; independent study in the lower-division courses seems to have created real interest in such work within departments, but this has tended to become an end in itself rather than a means of preparation for more extended work under the university plan. Actually the students who engage in independent study receive more individual guidance than those in regular courses, but most students prefer routine work, and for many pre-professional students courses are necessarily standardized. There have been only about 125 graduates under the university plan but those who have undertaken it and the members of the faculty who have directed and examined their work have been enthusiastic over the results. A high standard has been maintained—in general the standard of graduate work— and the value of the experience as a preparation for postgraduate study has been noteworthy. About three-quarters of the students who are graduated under this plan go on to postgraduate study. Many more students have undertaken independent work in connection with courses in the lower division (100-200 each year) mainly in the general Freshman course, "History of Western Civilization."

Teaching under the university independent study plan is mainly by weekly individual tutorial conferences. Examinations are oral and are held at the conclusion of the independent work undertaken; they are planned individually for each student.

In his report on independent study in the lower division, published by the Stanford University Press in 1937, Professor Edgar E. Robinson makes these significant comments: (1) that their whole experience has shown the marked disadvantages of exclusively classroom instruction for the superior student, (2) that students of high quality released from routine have set new standards of achievement, and (3) that, more important still, the effect of this work upon students and teachers alike has been to create a new attitude toward college work which influences directly or indirectly the whole community. These comments would, I think, find an approving echo in every college and university where independent study for superior students has been sincerely tried.[2]

[2] Readers who wish fuller details of honors work at Stanford should consult E. E. Robinson's two reports: *Independent Study at Stanford* and *Independent Study in the Lower Division at Stanford University*, Stanford University Press, 1937.

Chapter Seven

HONORS WORK ON A FULL-TIME BASIS

For maximum simplicity and effectiveness an honors plan should occupy the entire time of the student in the Junior and Senior years. For the honors student the course and credit system should cease to exist. He should be free to concentrate upon the task of mastering as thoroughly as possible the field of knowledge to be covered and his degree should depend upon success in his comprehensive examinations. The field of study should be wider than a single department and for the conduct of such a plan two or three departments should co-operate.

In a few institutions such co-operation between departments has been achieved, but in most places departmental feeling is too strong to make it possible. The excessive departmentalization of our undergraduate colleges is one of their greatest evils. Plans of independent study, therefore, which involve co-operation between departments, leaving each to do its best but planning to make their studies complement each other in the training of the student, offer an ideal method of breaking down departmental barriers. In the few institutions where such plans are in force the benefits accrue not merely to the student, but also to the members of the departments concerned.

Honors work at Swarthmore College, described in Chapter IV, is of this type. Other similar plans are those in force at the Massachusetts Institute of Technology, the University of Rochester, Smith College, the University of Virginia, and in certain programs at Princeton. The two-unit plan at Mt. Holyoke is essentially similar. Honors work at Rice Institute, Boston College, and Holy Cross, though somewhat differently organized, is also conducted on a full time basis. This chapter is devoted to a description of eight of these plans; the program at the University of Virginia will be considered in the chapter on state universities.

The honors course plan at the Massachusetts Institute of Technology (now suspended for the duration of the war) was for many years confined to the electrical engineering course. The mechanical and chemical engineering departments have now established honors courses with minor variations adapted to these particular fields. Honors work was begun in 1925 in electrical engineering under the leadership of Professor Dugald C. Jackson. An engineering "course," so-called at M.I.T., is broader than a single department; electrical engineering includes mathematics, physics, mechanics, thermodynamics, hydraulics, and other subjects. The honors plan at M.I.T. is not merely an addition to regular courses but replaces them so that the plan is a good illustration of the principles outlined at the beginning of this chapter. At the end of the Sophomore year, students in electrical engineering receive a letter explaining the plan, outlining the requirements for admission to it, and inviting those who are interested to apply. Selections are carefully made; the qualities sought are superior records, maturity, capacity for sound reasoning, initiative and sense of responsibility, and generally an analytic mind. Practically all the exceptional students in Course VI apply for admission to honors work. The selections are well made and any individual selected who proves in practice not to possess qualifications needed for success may be returned to a regular section.

The honors-group students are excused from laboratory discipline in the same sense that they are excused from classroom discipline; that is, they are not given specific, detailed, routine assignments, but are left to find their own problems and carry out the experimentation in a more original and reliant fashion than is expected of other students. The problems which they are encouraged to attack are not necessarily typical problems in the sense that they are problems of the type readily encountered, the solutions for which fall into well-known and easily determined patterns. In general, the problems attempted by honors-group students, both experimentally and analytically, are supposed to be of a more comprehensive character and to involve somewhat less usual situations than the simpler and more restricted problems that are presented in regular sections. Members of the honors group attend a weekly seminar which, in the Junior year, emphasizes definite mastery of the required subjects, and in the Senior year is devoted to the solution of broad engineering problems. Other departments which touch electrical engineering co-operate in providing a free and flexible program for honors students. Where the honors group from electrical engineering is sufficiently large, a given department may hold a special seminar for them. Otherwise they receive individual advice and their progress is discussed in interdepartmental conferences.

The comprehensive examinations by which honors work in electrical engineering is tested are severe and at the same time so interesting as to have definite educational value. They are set by a committee which includes three members from other engineering schools and from industry, together with two members of the M.I.T. staff not from the department of electrical engineering, and a chairman who is a member of that department. They cover the whole subject of electrical engineering as a professional field, last for two weeks, are both oral and written, and involve certain broad problems for the solution of which the student is free to use his own books and those in the library. While the examination is broad in scope, care is taken to set questions which require a deeper understanding of the basic principles of electrical engineering than would be the case in the term examinations for ordinary students(No formal honors are given at commencement; but apparently interest in honors work has not been diminished by the fact that it is left to be its own reward.)

As a result of a two-year study of the problem of the undergraduate program and the needs of abler and more ambitious students, the faculty of the University of(Rochester) inaugurated in 1939 an (admirable honors program which entirely replaces course work in the Junior and Senior years) Students are admitted at the end of the Sophomore year. Admission depends upon the candidate's ability to show a superior academic record and to convince the faculty that he has the initiative and intellectual interests necessary to enable him to succeed in independent work. For the honors student all course requirements are abolished. He attends instead eight seminars, two each semester, in from two to four fields. Although each student must take enough work in some single department to constitute a major study, there is less insistence at Rochester than in some other colleges that all the seminars be in related fields. This balance between heavy concentration and wide distribution has pleased the students who have been admitted to the division of honors studies. At the end of his Senior year each honors student must take a written and an oral examination, set by outside examiners, on the field

covered in each of his eight seminars. The outside examiners
are normally from other institutions; occasionally a member
of the Rochester faculty who has not taught a given student
serves as his examiner.

The number of students in the division of honors studies is
at present fortunately small. Growth will be much more solid
if it is gradual. A slow development will also allow time to
solve some local problems. One of these is the New York
State Board of Education requirement for a teaching certifi-
cate, which now makes it very difficult for some of the ablest
women to do honors work. Another is the rather rigid
curriculum requirements in most of the science departments
which have made it for the time being impossible for students
to do honors work in those fields. In one or two other departments the honors program is complicated by certain necessary
course prerequisites. Individual problems of this kind occur
in every institution; they are always difficult but, given sufficient good will, never insolvable.

Although the honors program has not been in operation
long enough at Rochester to make possible any definitive judgment of its success, it has clearly been intellectually stimulating to the students in the division; it has also had a helpful, if
intangible, effect on some of those who have continued in
course work. The instructors who have conducted honors
seminars are enthusiastic about the method and its results, and
in the faculty there is whole-hearted approval of the new
program.[1]

[1] The author has had the privilege of seeing a similar plan drawn
up by the Executive Committee for the A.B. degree of Trinity College,
which recommends the establishment of an honors program based on the
principles underlying the various plans described in this chapter. The
recommendations are in brief that for honors candidates the course-credit
system be abolished, that honors seminars (and where desired a Senior
thesis) should entirely supersede course work in the Junior and Senior
years, that degrees be awarded on the basis of comprehensive examinations,

The experience of Smith College is interesting because of the fact that the college has maintained for twenty years two honors plans: general honors for which independent work has been allowed to replace one course, and special honors for which independent study is substituted for the entire program of instruction in courses. The Smith faculty has not been satisfied with the working of either plan, and has lately been engaged in revising them and formulating a new program. I had the privilege of participating in the discussions which led to the inauguration of the two plans twenty years ago, and have lately spent an evening with the members of the Smith faculty reviewing their experience and considering the form which a new plan might take. (The experience of Smith College bears out all that is said in this volume as to the superiority of an honors plan which takes the entire time of the student during the Senior and Junior years, over one in which the time and effort of the undergraduate are divided between independent study and regular course work.) The experiments with the two plans at the same institution make this result conclusive. In trying it out so thoroughly and in assessing so frankly the results, the members of the Smith faculty have done a service to all colleges and universities which are concerned with this idea.

The dissatisfaction of the Smith faculty with their special honors plan, which takes the entire time of the student for the last two years, should not blind the outside observer to its substantial merits. It has for many years offered to ambitious undergraduates the opportunity for thorough and independent work which could not possibly be found in the con-

---

set by external examiners, covering the entire two years of honors work. This bold and well-conceived plan is interesting on its own account and also as an example of the way in which colleges and universities are in these days making plans for the improvement of the liberal arts curriculum after the war.

ventional course system. I know this not merely from members of the Smith College faculty but also from graduates who have worked under this plan. Undoubtedly honors work at Smith has lost something from the fact that the College has not, during the last twenty years, used external examiners, which are needed for the best results. The plan has furthermore suffered from the fact that it has been so largely departmentalized and has, therefore, allowed undue specialization, though there was nothing in the plan itself to make that inevitable. It will not usually be best for an American undergraduate to spend the entire time of his Junior and Senior years in one department. Where the student is allowed to give his entire time to honors work, as he should for the best results, it is important that his program be arranged in co-operation between two or three departments.

In colleges and universities organized on a departmental basis, as are ours in the United States, this co-operation between departments is not easy to achieve. On the other hand it is not impossible. Perhaps the simplest device for securing the desired result is an organization by divisions such as obtains at Swarthmore and at Harvard. If then the work of a given student is done in two or three subjects in the same division the result will be a program not too narrowly specialized and at the same time not too widely scattered. Such a modification of the special honors program at Smith would, I believe, eliminate most of the causes of dissatisfaction which students and members of the faculty feel with it at present. To the general principle of providing for the best students a freer and more severe program than would be suitable for those of average ability, the Smith faculty has been committed under the leadership of President Neilson, and the general principles upon which such work should be based have never been better stated than in the inaugural address delivered by President Davis when he succeeded President Neilson in 1940. We may expect that in such a favorable environment a satisfactory plan will soon be put into operation.

Princeton has been a pioneer in breaking the academic lock step. Since 1905 there has been a steadily increasing effort to give individual treatment to all students. While there is no general university plan of honors work, certain divisions, schools, and departments have taken advantage of the flexibility in course requirements which applies to all undergraduates to put into force programs limited to the best and the most ambitious. These programs combine courses, theses, independent reading, and comprehensive examinations in such a way as to offer admirable training for those students who possess the needed ability and intellectual initiative. It is to be hoped that the success of the programs now in operation will lead to their further extension.

I shall sketch first the general university regulations which apply to students of all levels of ability and then describe the use which has been made of this freedom to provide special opportunities for the best. The rigid course system has been modified at Princeton for all students in several ways: by the preceptorial which, since its establishment in 1905, has given a great impetus to tutorial work throughout the country; by the arrangements for departmental specialization replacing the old system of majors and minors; by the so-called four course plan for Seniors and Juniors under which students are expected to do the work which would correspond to a fifth course by directed independent study in the department of their choice; by the "no-course" plan under which high-ranking students are entirely relieved of course requirements in the second term of the Senior year and allowed to concentrate all their efforts upon independent study and the writing of a thesis; by general comprehensive examinations; and by the introduction of a reading period at the end of each semester, which, however, is in abeyance for the duration of the war.

Under the system of departmental specialization the student becomes in his Junior year an "undergraduate member of his department" and his work is planned and directed for the last two years by the department through the agency of a supervisor. The plan encourages a high degree of concentration and has had the result of giving the best students what has aptly been termed a professional attitude toward their work. This attitude is greatly strengthened by the requirement of Senior theses, some of which are good enough to be published in journals of learned societies. Comprehensive examinations are set by each department acting as a whole, and stress the subject in its entirety instead of being limited to the content of individual courses. For graduation the comprehensive examination is given a definite numerical rating and is averaged with the student's grades in departmental courses, on his thesis, and on his independent study. Honors are awarded on the basis of the student's thesis plus his showing in the comprehensive examinations. For honors, grades in courses are not counted. Every student is theoretically a candidate for honors, and the awards are made on the basis of tests which are the same for all.

Taking advantage of the freedom allowed under these regulations, the Division of the Humanities has put into operation a divisional program confined to high-ranking students leading to divisional as well as to departmental honors. Students admitted to this program work under supervision throughout the entire four years of their college course. The program offers to those qualified for it the opportunity for an adventure in study and thinking which could not be offered by any system of courses alone. The selection of students for this plan begins in June preceding the entrance of Freshmen in September. School records of the entering students are studied by the divisional committee and those Freshmen whose abilities and interests seem to qualify them are invited to call on the chairman of the committee during the first week of term. In normal times sixty or seventy respond, and of these the most promising are selected and are assigned to a particular supervisor. After the first year the students are guided in their work by the member of the Humanistic Committee who represents the department of their choice as well as by the committee as a whole. From the beginning the student has his choice of courses carefully supervised in order that he may be induced to elect an integrated program of study and to explore the relationship between the subject matter of his different courses. In his first year the student takes foundation courses in the general field of the humanities as well as distribution courses in the natural and social sciences, one or two of which will be of Sophomore level. In the Sophomore and Junior years each student takes four upperclass courses in his department and at the end of the Junior year he takes most of his Senior comprehensive examinations. Having thus completed at the end of his Junior year most of the requirements for graduation, the student embarks in his Senior year upon an ambitious program of independent reading and advanced courses focused upon the field of his thesis. He works under the direction of the Humanistic Committee and at the end of his Senior year takes the remaining portion of his Senior comprehensive examinations and in addition a comprehensive examination set especially for each student for both departmental and divisional honors; departmental honors are awarded on the basis of departmental comprehensive examinations and thesis, divisional honors on the basis of the final divisional examination and the thesis.

Throughout their entire college course the students following this plan meet at intervals for conferences on the subject matter of their work. The departments combined in this program are art and archaeology, history, philosophy, English, classics, modern languages, and religion. Representatives from the natural sciences, politics, and economics serve on the divisional committee of the humanities as associate members.

The department of chemistry, while scrupulously adhering to the university policy of giving individual attention to all students, has likewise taken advantage of the freedom of the general requirements to institute a special program for those of highest ability. Here again selections begin on the basis of records in preparatory school. Freshman and Sophomore classes are sectioned on the basis of ability (as are classes in most departments of the university) and early in their first year all Freshmen who have previously studied chemistry take an elementary but comprehensive examination, the results of which enable the staff to make a more accurate segregation of the best. Certain special courses in the first two years are open only to the best students and are of distinctly more advanced character. For students in the Junior year the department has recently established the so-called Junior *colloquium*, a weekly meeting for the discussion of problems in the field of chemistry. A topic for each meeting is assigned in advance and students are expected to read up on the subject as much as possible beforehand. The department supervises during the Junior and Senior years independent work by all students in accordance with the general university plan.

Integrated programs to which admission is selective on the basis of ability are likewise offered in the Creative Arts, in American Civilization, and in the School of Public and International Affairs. The Program of Study in American Civilization is primarily an upperclass program, and is administered by a committee of representatives chosen from six co-operating departments—art and archaeology, English, philosophy, history, politics, and economics. Thus, unlike the other two Princeton programs, it integrates the humanities with the social studies. Furthermore, students enrolled in the program do not study American civilization in isolation, but on the contrary are required to investigate American institutions and ideas in relation to those of the other countries with which the United States has been in contact.

A student formally enrolls in the Program in his Junior year and is also enrolled in one of the six co-operating departments. He pursues the regular course of study in the department of his choice, though stressing the American aspects of his departmental work. In addition, he must elect during his last two years at least four courses in the American field outside of his own department. Of these courses, one must be historical in its method of approach, one must deal with American political or social institutions, one must be philosophical or systematic in its method, and the fourth must be concerned with American art or literature.

In his last year the student participates in a conference which investigates a problem of fundamental importance in American civilization by means of supervised independent study, round-table discussions, written reports, and special lectures by experts, many of whom come from outside the University. It is with respect to the conference that the Program of Study in American Civilization becomes for students of high rank essentially an honors program, for in normal times only such students are allowed to participate fully in the conference. In the case of these students particular emphasis is placed on independent research, which is carried on individually and co-operatively. These students are also given special access to the visiting lecturers.

The School of Public and International Affairs differs from the Humanistic and American Civilization programs in that its students have no other departmental ties. Fifty men from each class, chosen on the basis of scholastic standing from a much larger number of applicants, are admitted to the School at the end of Sophomore year. Each one, under the direction of the School staff, frames a program of study to meet his own particular needs and interests. The students are encouraged to develop special fields of their own, so long as they fall within the general field of public affairs. In his Senior year each student takes comprehensive examinations and writes a thesis under the direction of the School staff. Many of these theses are the results of field work done in the United States or abroad on scholarships granted to students during the summer following the Junior year.

The central feature in the School's work is the conference on public affairs. In this course the students are assigned a broad problem of public policy, upon which they work during the term. They organize and conduct the investigation themselves, with the assistance of the conference staff, and each student presents his findings on one phase of the subject at one of a series of formal sessions. Outside investigation through field trips and interviews is emphasized and to some extent financed by the School.

The two-unit plan at Mt. Holyoke is a well-conceived plan of independent study limited to students with mature intellectual interests and sufficient independence and initiative to profit by the adventures in learning which the plan offers. It is not called an honors program, but it has much in common with the plans described in this chapter. It goes further than most full-time plans of honors work in that it removes course requirements and provides tutorial guidance for independent study during all four years of work for the bachelor's degree. The student selects her subjects with the aid of an adviser on the basis of her own individual interests. Great emphasis is laid on the intimate association of the students with one another and with members of the faculty. Those working under this plan may or may not try for honors. A large proportion of them is likely to be elected to Phi Beta Kappa. Mt. Holyoke maintains in addition a plan of honors work replacing twelve hours out of thirty in the Senior year. Students receive their instruction by the tutorial method or in seminars. They are required to write a thesis and to undergo a special examination in addition to the general examination required of all students.

The plans in force at Rice Institute, Boston College, and Holy Cross resemble those previously described in this chapter in that the student devotes all or nearly all of his time to honors work. They differ from them, however, in that they keep the course system intact. The student does his work in special honors classes, open only to superior students, which replace the regular curriculum.

Since its foundation in 1916 Rice Institute has offered honors courses in the Junior and Senior years limited to students who have made high grades in the first two years and who desire a greater degree of specialization than is provided by the ordinary curriculum. The opportunity is extended to not more than ten per cent of the two upper classes. Honors courses are offered in most departments but not in all. The standard maintained is high and both students and members of the faculty are enthusiastic about honors work. While the work is carried on in courses, those designed for honors students require more outside work, which the student must do independently, than do the regular courses at the Institute. The plan is modest but sincerely and thoroughly administered, and its success has been tested by the experience of more than a quarter of a century.

The honors plans at the Jesuit institutions, of which Boston College and Holy Cross are two examples, differ from those usually in force in several respects. Students are admitted to honors work earlier, at entrance in the case of Boston College and at the end of the first year at Holy Cross. Honors work is furthermore confined to students in the liberal arts, who under present rules must have a good foundation in classics. At St. Louis University the honors plan has been extended to other subjects and it is possible that the same thing may happen at Boston College and Holy Cross, where many of the best students are at present excluded from the honors program because of the Greek requirement.

Teaching at these two institutions is largely in special sections, limited to honors students, which go faster and further than the courses in the same subjects for ordinary students. Both at Boston College and at Holy Cross a high standard of work is required and students who do not meet that standard are transferred to the regular course. Shrinkage due to this cause may amount to as much as fifty per cent. The programs are rigid in both institutions, although a few electives are allowed. In elective courses the honors student is expected to do more than ordinary students in the same course. Honors work at the Jesuit colleges is conducted with all the care and pedagogical skill for which these institutions are famous. It is an admirable adaptation of the principle of special facilities for the best students to the framework of Roman Catholic education.

(The advantages of allowing honors work to replace completely course requirements in the Junior and Senior years are obvious. The attention of the student is not distracted by the effort to live up to different and sometimes conflicting requirements. He can concentrate upon one task; he need not leave the library or the laboratory to attend a lecture; he need not interrupt the preparation of an original paper to study a lesson in a textbook. His work may be harder but it is simpler and he is free to give it all his energy and all his ability.

If his two final years are devoted to subjects in two or three related departments, in which he has already taken elementary courses in his first two years, his work will not be too narrowly specialized, although it will be focused upon a single field. His reading in one subject will illuminate his study of another. He will not merely acquire information but will also begin to understand for himself the relationship of ideas. His knowledge will have not only breadth but also unity. He will begin to experience the feeling of mastery which is the strongest lure to further achievement.)

CHAPTER EIGHT

THE THREEFOLD PROBLEM OF THE STATE UNIVERSITIES

(IN THE state universities, and in some other institutions as well, the task of providing special facilities for students of higher than average ability is made at once more urgent and more difficult because of the presence of a considerable body of students whose ability to do university work is distinctly below the average.) Just as the average students tend to pull down the level of the work of the best, if all are taught together, so do the members of the lower group constitute a threat to the average standard. Most state universities are required by law to admit graduates from public high schools within the state. As a rule, though there are of course many exceptions, students who rank in the lower half of their class in high school are not qualified to succeed in college work. Such students are usually excluded by colleges and universities with limited enrollment and an excess of applicants, but they may enter the Freshman class of their state university without question. Furthermore, many colleges which depend largely on tuition fees and have fewer applicants for admission than they would like, find it practically impossible to refuse any high-school graduate. Indeed some colleges may be forced to go even further and admit with conditions students who have not succeeded in all their high-school studies and hence cannot qualify for admission to the state university. As a result regimentation, which is an evil under any circumstances, has more serious consequences in such colleges and in the state universities than anywhere else. The faculties of the stronger state institutions are keenly aware of this threefold problem. No fewer than twenty-two maintain plans of honors work for superior students and several have in recent years undertaken to provide a special course for those who are not qualified to succeed in ordinary work. The purpose of this chapter is to examine these interesting plans.

It is difficult for large institutions to experiment, to follow any but well-trodden paths, and particularly difficult to persuade state legislators to appropriate funds for a program of this type, limited to the few, when they find it hard enough to supply the needs of the many. Under these circumstances it is all the more creditable that honors plans are in operation in a number of our stronger state institutions and that two at least, Virginia and Ohio, have taken positions of leadership in the movement. The admirable program conducted at the University of Virginia belongs in the category discussed in the preceding chapter, since it replaces entirely the course and hour system in the Junior and Senior years. The Ohio plan is essentially similar to the group discussed in Chapter VI in that independent study is allowed to displace only a part of the regular course work, but it is different in other respects, indeed it is unique in the way in which the honors plan is grafted on the roots of the course and hour system.

The University of Virginia is one of the oldest and most conservative of our state institutions and not one of the richest. These facts make it all the more remarkable that Virginia should have developed an honors plan which, while it does not affect all departments (or schools, as they are called in Jefferson's phrase) and reaches as yet only a small proportion of the student body, is nevertheless thoroughgoing and well conceived. There is a regulation which permits groups of two or more schools or departments to combine to formulate an honors program, but this has not as yet been acted on in practice. On the other hand, the word "subject" is broadly used and may embrace the field of more than one school or department. Thus, an honors program sponsored by one department may involve a request by the department to a professor in another to give the student concerned tutorial instruction. If the faculty of the University of Virginia builds upon the foundations which have been so well laid the result will be an outstanding example of the possibility of the adaptation of the honors idea to the conditions of a state university.

(Virginia has made the conditions for entering honors work extremely severe, seeking quality rather than numbers.) The chairman of the honors committee studies the records of the students in their second year in the University to determine the high-standing men. Those interested in honors work are invited to an informal interview with the chairman and on the twofold basis of academic record and personal qualifications honors students are chosen.

A plan of study for the Junior and Senior years is made out by the major department in consultation with the student and this plan must receive the approval of the faculty committee on degrees with honors. Once accepted the plan becomes both the basis for the student's work and a guide for setting his final comprehensive examination. There is some difference between departments as to the scope of honors work. The method of teaching is usually by individual tutorials, although here also procedure varies. Final examinations are set by outside examiners or by members of the Virginia faculty who have had no part in teaching the student who is being examined. They include both written papers and an oral.

All degrees with honors must be recommended to the faculty by the honors committee. Some member of the committee follows closely the examination of each student, the reports of the examiners in all departments are considered, and after careful discussion degrees are recommended. The plan seems to have been admirably thought out in all its details. It is carefully administered by the Committee on Degrees with Honors rather than by departments, and its prospects of success are all the brighter for the fact that the number of students in the early years has been small so that every problem and every difficulty could receive individual attention.

(The honors program at Ohio State University is a triumph of educational statesmanship in its effective use of the conventional course and credit system for the purpose of giving to abler and more ambitious students the freer and more severe program which they need and which the conventional system usually makes impossible.\ The honors committee of the College of Arts and Sciences at Ohio State adopted what they called a realistic policy. They believed it to be out of the question to find time or funds for any system of tutorial or individual instruction, and they felt that no honors plan would endure which was not rooted in the prevailing course system. They found in the program of certain departments courses of variable content bearing such titles as "Special Topics," "Minor Problems," "Honors Reading," and the like, the subject matter of which might be determined by the instructor and to some extent by the interests of the students who enrolled each quarter. Most of these courses have a flexible credit provision and may count for from three to ten hours per quarter according to the amount and quality of the work done by each individual. In these courses the committee found a device which functioned freely in the course and hour system and which could be used to accomplish the results of individual tutorial instruction. Through the efforts of the committee the number of these courses was gradually increased until they are offered in twenty-seven different fields. Each honors student is required to enroll in the appropriate course and to do independent work under the direction of the professor in charge, who acts, so to speak, as his tutor. The student may thus spend approximately half his time on honors work.

The standard for admission to honors work is unusually high (half A's and half B's in the first two years) and the honors program is, and is intended to be, much more severe than work in ordinary courses. Success is tested by a comprehensive examination at the end of the Senior year, which may be both written and oral and in any case must include an oral examination of at least one hour in length. In one year nine per cent of the Senior class took the degree with distinction (as the honors degree is called); in normal years nearly one-half of those whose records make them eligible actually do their Junior and Senior work under this plan. Honors work has made steady progress in spite of some objection and some indifference; it has the happy characteristic of involving no additional drain on the university budget. As Professor Royall Snow has said: "It costs nothing except intelligence."

Recently Ohio State University has carried further this program of segregating students of unusual academic promise by restricting certain sections of the large Freshman courses to students who stood in the top ten per cent of their class in high school or who had made a creditable showing in placement examinations. Both students and members of the faculty are enthusiastic about the effects of this plan and the quality of the work done under it.

Aside from Virginia and Ohio twenty other state universities have taken definite steps in the direction of honors work. The schemes differ in different places, but they resemble on the whole the plans described in Chapter VI. Examples are Colorado, Kansas, Maine, Michigan, and Minnesota.

The honors system at the University of Colorado has been in existence since 1930. Until 1941 chief emphasis was on broadening the range of the student's knowledge rather than improving his grasp of his major field. This plan has recently been modified to provide for departmental honors only, for the duration of the war. This modification is considered experimental and the whole problem of the organization of honors work will be reviewed at the end of the war. Interest is keen on the part of both faculty and students, and with the experience accumulated it may be expected that the University of Colorado will evolve a plan combining the two ideals of breadth and thoroughness.

The University of Kansas maintains a departmental honors plan, started in 1931 partly as a result of interest aroused in the minds of Kansas professors who had served as examiners at Park College, and a general honors plan open to students who have already qualified for departmental honors. Teaching is in so-called honors courses. Examinations are set by members of the faculty who have not taught the student who is being examined. The number of students so far affected is small, but many members of the faculty are keenly interested. One committee report which I had the privilege of reading sums up admirably the arguments in favor of honors work and recommends a more thoroughgoing plan.

At the University of Maine honors work replaces one course during the Junior and Senior years. Preparatory courses in the study of the world's great classics are offered in the Sophomore year. In the Junior year honors work consists of preparation of a broad field, and the Senior year is devoted to intensive study of some particular topic in this field. A thesis is required. Instruction is by the tutorial method, and the work is tested by comprehensive examinations covering the student's work of his entire four years. There is keen faculty interest, and the majority of the best students do honors work.

At the University of Michigan an independent reading group, started fifteen years ago, laid the foundation for the present greatly improved honors plan which was started in September, 1939. Honors work may replace one-third of the regularly required classes in the Junior and Senior years. Teaching is by individual tutorials or seminars, as the case may be. Students must write a thesis and undergo a comprehensive examination at the end of the Senior year. This examination covers the regular courses they have taken as well as their honors work. The plan is too recent to have made great headway, but it is supported by a group of real enthusiasts in the faculty.

At the University of Minnesota interest has long been keen in the provision of special facilities for students of various levels of ability. The so-called General College for students below the average is described later in this chapter. A "university college" is, I am told, now being planned for superior students. At the present moment special honors courses are offered, open only to students with high records in connection with which some tutorial supervision is provided. Because of real interest of both students and members of the faculty, a significant program may eventually be expected.

At the Universities of California, Illinois, Indiana, Iowa, Missouri, Nebraska, New Mexico, North Carolina, North Dakota, Oklahoma, Tennessee, Texas, Vermont, Washington, and Wisconsin some provision over and above the regular curriculum is made for the needs of students of superior ability. These vary from opportunity for extra work in addition to regular course requirements to plans of the type described in the preceding paragraphs. In several universities, as at California, certain courses are limited to high-ranking students and offer the opportunity for freer and more individual work. In most of the universities mentioned, honors work is strictly departmentalized, and in several of them high-ranking undergraduates are admitted to graduate courses. Personal supervision of independent work in seminars or individual tutorials is almost universal. While the arrangements now provided leave much to be desired, they do indicate that members of the faculties of the leading state universities are aware of the problem and have taken some steps to meet it.

Certainly the results so far achieved by honors work in all but a few of the state universities are modest, but, in view of the difficulties, the interest in the subject is encouraging. The greatest of these difficulties is the presence of so large a group of students for whom even the average standards of course work are too severe. It is not to be expected that special facilities for superior students can be provided in our state institutions unless at the same time steps are taken to meet the needs of these individuals of less than average capacity. This is entirely reasonable and the advocates of honors plans have nothing to gain and everything to lose by neglecting the interests of those individuals who stand at the other end of the academic scale. The problem of what to do for them is difficult, but it is being courageously attacked in a few state universities. The interesting details of these plans fall outside the scope of this volume but a few words about their leading features and the principles involved will complete the picture.

The leader, by common consent, has been the University of Minnesota. Obliged by its charter to accept all students who are certified by accredited public high schools, the University is attempting loyally and intelligently to discover and provide the kind of environment which will enable as many as possible of these individuals to develop their powers to the fullest degree. The honors plan for Juniors and Seniors previously described, now in the process of revision, is one contribution toward the solution of this problem; the General College, established in 1935 for students who lack the intellectual interests needed to enable them to succeed in the ordinary University program, is another. Some of these students come to the University with high-school records so low as to make it unlikely that they can do work up to the average standard. Some have transferred from other institutions but have failed to qualify for advanced standing at the University of Minnesota; some have been transferred from other departments of the University. A certain percentage show average or higher than average ability but find that the courses offered in the General College better suit their needs than those offered in the regular four-year curriculum; some can afford only two years of university work and prefer a program complete in itself rather than half of a four-year course.

The General College has a small faculty of its own and additional needed instruction is given by the members of regular University departments. Survey courses predominate, but the emphasis is upon human activities rather than upon the organization of subject matter by scholars. The work of the two years leads to the degree of "Associate in Arts." No one who knows American education will underestimate the difficulty of making a success of a program of this character. The Minnesota faculty considers the progress made so far rather as a first step in a research program than as a finally complete solution of the problem.

Ohio State University has attacked the problem of the

academic misfit in the same spirit in which the faculty evolved its interesting honors program. Since 1934 both University committees and committees of the College of Arts and Sciences have made a thorough study of the whole problem. It was discovered that three types of students need special attention: (1) students who enter the University with limited preparation for regular curricula; (2) students who are undecided in their academic plans; (3) competent students who do not plan to remain in the University longer than six quarters.

To the College of Arts and Sciences was assigned the responsibility of preparing programs for these groups of students. For the students with limited or unsatisfactory preparation a remedial, tutorial, and advisory program has been established. For undecided students an exploratory program with a complete testing service is offered and for the temporary students a program of General Education. In this two-year program of General Education fifteen courses, entitled General Studies, have been prepared. In a broad, introductory way they cover the languages, the natural sciences, the social sciences, the humanities, and the area of applied psychology. The remedial, exploratory, and General Education programs are under the direction of the Junior Dean and are a part of the faculty advisory plan of the College.

The success of the movement to provide special facilities for those who fall below the average or who lack the intellectual interests needed for the ordinary liberal arts program promises not merely to safeguard our average standard of achievement, which is threatened by the regimentation of these students with other groups, but also to strengthen the case for the provision of better opportunities for the best. The efforts which are now being made to provide for students of modest ability a sound and worth-while program suited to their capacity are an important part of this nation-wide effort to develop to the utmost all the students in all our colleges and universities.)

(In no field of higher education is experimentation more needed than in providing the best training for students of less than average ability.) To avoid clumsy circumlocutions we apply the terms better and poorer, superior and inferior, more and less able, to the various groups of students whose needs are discussed in this volume, but at the same time we must face the fact that such terms tend to confuse the issue. The most important differences between them are frequently in their interests and purposes in life. Many students do badly the tasks set for them in college courses because they see no meaning in these tasks, no promise of aid in developing themselves into the kind of men and women they hope to be, and no preparation for the kind of work which they intend to do in the world. In this attitude the students are frequently right and it is our regimented college system which is at fault.

There are many ways of getting an education, and one of the best is to get it from the work which a man or woman does to earn a living. Many young people instinctively feel this; what they seek is training to do that work well, and, perhaps unconsciously, some idea of the relation of the occupation they expect to enter to the great ends of civilization. A man or woman who understands his place in the scheme of national life has an education which so far as it goes is liberal and will contribute to his peace and happiness.

(For many occupations a four-year academic training is unnecessary and may even be a handicap. Students who are listless and ineffective in their attack upon the abstract subjects of the conventional college curriculum will often be keenly interested in vocational studies and do excellent work in them.)

The so-called terminal curricula offered in junior colleges meet this need and the success of students in these courses shows that they provide an answer to many seemingly insoluble problems of students who fail in college. Courses of this character may be more expensive to offer than elementary mathematics and languages; they demand skill and experience on the part of the teacher. They cannot be taught part time by young candidates for the Ph.D. Well done they may become an enormously important part of our system of higher education.

For many technical occupations and semi-professions high schools offer too little training and technical schools of engineering, agriculture, medicine, and the like, too much. These include practical farm work, a large number of specialized activities in connection with business and engineering, the application of the fine arts to interior decoration and costume design, various laboratory posts, home economics, stenography, and many forms of public service for which practical rather than theoretical training is essential.

There is, furthermore, an approach to liberal studies which may have value even though it does not provide the thorough foundation necessary for advanced and specialized knowledge. This approach is illustrated by special elementary courses sometimes offered by departments for students who are specializing in other fields and who must content themselves with only one course. It is illustrated less well perhaps by the knowledge obtained from orientation courses and by the many popular handbooks designed to explain the various sciences to laymen. For the student who does not expect to become a scholar, whose main interest is in some practical job, and who will get the discipline he needs from the study and practice of his vocation, such an approach to the liberal arts may have great educative value. In these and other ways the courses in junior colleges and the special courses in state universities leading after two years to the degree of Associate in Arts are opening up a whole new field of education, supplying a need which neither the high school, the ordinary liberal arts college, nor the technical and professional schools can meet.

This problem confronts most insistently the junior colleges and the state universities, but it is not confined to them. Many small colleges, as indicated above, are able to maintain no higher entrance requirements than those imposed by law upon the state universities. Some colleges cannot even do that. They must accept with conditions students who have not succeeded in fulfilling all the requirements for graduation from a public high school. The best interests of democracy will be served not by excluding these students, but rather by arranging the right program for them. It seems possible that the lead taken by a group of state universities in the attack on this problem may set a useful example for many small colleges and for junior colleges all over the country. An intelligent and workable solution would provide for a group which, when not specially cared for, tends to pull down the standards of the average, and it would beyond that constitute a great contribution to democratic education.

Breaking the academic lock step, distinguishing between the needs and capabilities of students of various levels of ability, may lead in the end to more intelligent and rigorous classification of universities and colleges than now exists. The list of institutions approved by the Association of American Universities is the most useful rating at the present time. The basis upon which it is made is clearly and publicly stated, and the requirements are enforced without fear or favor. The lists of the various regional associations, although less rigorous, have their own value, while the committee on qualifications for Phi Beta Kappa has during the last few years been making notably intelligent and fearless estimates of the qualifications of colleges and universities proposed for membership. Outside all these groups there are hundreds of institutions calling themselves colleges and universities, licensed by their state Boards of Education to confer degrees, which enjoy no recognition from regularly organized educational associations. In some cases this is due to the fact that the institution in question, while of good quality, is not so organized as to fit into any conventional niche. In most cases lack of recognition is due to poverty of resources, lack of library and laboratory facilities, and mediocre quality in the faculty and student body.

This study is based upon inspection of work in institutions which have received recognition by being placed on the approved list of the Association of American Universities. Even among these institutions the disparity in scholarship, in resources, in quality of faculty and student body is astounding. It has been suggested that our whole American educational system would be improved if groups of weak institutions could be induced to pool their resources to make fewer and stronger ones. While doubtless desirable, this does not seem very likely to happen. No human organization is more tenacious of life than a college or university. However weak it may be, it is a business asset and a source of pride to the community in which it is located. It is frequently valued as the embodiment of the doctrines of some religious denomination. It enjoys the uncritical loyalty (uncritical, that is, as to intellectual quality) of its alumni. It may always achieve, by methods universally understood, a cheap prominence on the athletic field, and an unctuous president may always deceive a certain part of the gullible public by excusing mediocre intellectual work on the ground that the main emphasis is placed not upon intellect but upon character.

While it is probably impossible to abolish the majority of these weaker colleges and universities, it ought to be possible to make them more useful. Their students will for the most part (but not entirely) belong to the lower third with which the state universities are at present making such an intelligent effort to deal. If these plans for a course leading to the degree of Associate in Arts achieve clear and unquestioned success, if the work which they offer attracts students and demonstrates its value for practical life, the inevitable rivalry for students will lead weaker colleges and universities to imitate these programs in which their chances for success would be so much greater than in regular undergraduate work.

If the state universities could see their way to becoming not merely teaching but also examining institutions for the degree of Associate in Arts, if they were prepared to confer this degree upon any student trained in any one of a not too narrowly selected list of colleges in their state, upon the passing of an appropriate examination set and conducted by the state university, they would solve the problem. With these possibilities before him the student could attend a minor college or a junior college and at the same time look forward to receiving a degree from the state university. His anxiety to succeed in the examinations set for this degree would make him a better student, interested in the improvement of intellectual standards of his institution, critical of bad teaching and of the wasteful expenditure of college funds upon buildings and miscellaneous activities instead of upon books and laboratories and professors. The morale of students and faculty in colleges of limited resources would be transformed by the challenge set by these examinations and the consequent opportunity of wider recognition. Just because this group of ill-prepared students is so large, just because so many local colleges and junior colleges must cater mainly to students of this grade, just because these students present so formidable a problem to the state universities, these universities, founded and supported by taxpayers' money, have the opportunity of so administering the degree of Associate in Arts as to bring a new strength and sincerity into the part of our educational system where those qualities are most needed.

CHAPTER NINE

THE ORGANIZATION OF INSTRUCTION AND EXAMINATIONS

MY PURPOSE in this and the following chapter is to draw together the various suggestions which have been made in the preceding pages concerning the organization and administration of honors work and, at the risk of a certain amount of repetition, to emphasize the lessons to be drawn from the various plans and procedures which have been described. It is highly desirable that many different experiments should be tried; if intelligent use is made of the experience so gained, great improvement in our methods should be possible. No single plan will work best in all places. On the other hand students and professors in one institution should not have to struggle helplessly against difficulties and handicaps which experience in others has shown to be avoidable. The most important questions here discussed are the general organization of honors work, problems connected with individual instruction, methods of examination, criticisms and objections, and the all-important problem of expense. This chapter will be confined to those questions which primarily concern the faculty—organization of honors plans and methods of teaching and examination—and the one following with problems which are the primary concern of the administration—criticisms, objections, and costs.

It is to be hoped that the part-time honors programs which are most widely used at present will constitute only a transition stage, and that more colleges and universities will be emboldened by success to allow honors work to replace completely the course and hour system in the Junior and Senior years. The simplicity of the full-time plan is in itself a great advantage. The honors student who is only partly occupied in independent study and must do part of his work in courses has not merely the problem of making a proper division of his time and energy; he is also divided in his attitude. He is less likely to acquire that mastery which comes from quiet brooding over the material on which he is engaged. Broken work is hard work and it is likely to destroy the atmosphere of leisurely concentration which is the most favorable condition for flashes of insight and understanding. The student misses the joy of being able to focus all his time and effort whole-heartedly upon one task.

Undergraduate life at its best contains too many distractions, but it can be unified by such a simplification of academic requirements as the full-time honors program implies. Every device which tends in the direction of such simplification has a good effect, so far as it goes: the point system, limiting participation in extra-curricular activities; the reduction of the regular program from five courses to four; the establishment of reading periods; long vacations in which the most ambitious undergraduates do the solid continuous work that in term time they are able only to map out. The best solution for the best students in our universities will be an organization of their honors work which will make it possible for them to concentrate all their time and energy upon one or two subjects, freed from the demands of the course and hour system, excused from the need of earning credits, dependent for their degree entirely upon the comprehensive examinations at the end of their course.)

(It will lend further emphasis and unity to honors work if the distinctions awarded at commencement time are dependent upon the results of honors examinations rather than upon course grades.) I have already pointed out how commencement honors and election to Phi Beta Kappa operate in some institutions to penalize honors work. It is not necessary that such distinctions be closed to students who take their degrees in courses. While a healthy and successful honors plan will eventually draw in most of the best students, a certain number of superior students will be unable, for one reason or another, to give up courses. Some of these will make outstanding records and should receive whatever recognition they are thought to deserve. (The important point is that honors work, which will and should be judged by a more severe standard than that which obtains in regular courses, should not be averaged in with course grades on any numerical basis.) All awards, whether to honors students or to course students, should be made by some estimate of what are thought to be the relative merits of the individual candidates. Comparisons between members of the two groups cannot be arithmetical, but may none the less be just, and fully as accurate as any numerical measures of human quality and promise are likely to be.

In the discussion of full-time plans the difficulty has already been pointed out of allowing a student to spend the entire time of two years on honors work confined to a single department; this implies specialization to a degree which most faculties believe undesirable for American undergraduates. The remedy is to (plan honors programs in fields embracing two or three related departments.) A convenient method of achieving this end is to group the departments of instruction into divisions, a practice which is already followed in many colleges and universities. The usual groupings are humanities, social studies, and mathematics and the natural sciences. Sometimes the scientific group is divided between the physical and the biological sciences. Subjects like mathematics, history, and philosophy should be included in more than one division. If then the honors student is allowed, after having fulfilled the general requirements of distribution in his first two years, to spend his last two years on two or three subjects chosen from the same division, he will have a program sufficiently broad to ensure a well-rounded education, and at the same time so focused upon a single field of knowledge as to make his work in one subject contribute to his understanding of another.

Most of the institutions undertaking honors work provide some kind of individual instruction. This may take the form of tutorials or of small seminars. In some institutions both forms have a place. (The seminar has grown so common as to promise to become the distinctive American contribution to the art of individual instruction.) I have already indicated in Chapter IV that from the first the Swarthmore faculty chose the seminar method of instruction rather than the individual tutorial. It seemed better adapted to the conditions of an American college and twenty years of experience have strengthened that belief. The popularity of this way of teaching in other colleges and universities offers further confirmation.

(The seminar method is so natural that it is hard to go wrong with it: the only things that will spoil it are, first, the presence of mediocre or ill-prepared students, and, second, a tendency on the part of any member, and especially of the professor in charge, to talk too much.) Given keen and able students and a teacher who will direct his efforts to bringing out their ideas, and given also a sense of leisure and absence of need to get on to the next engagement, success is almost automatic. The degrees of success, however, are infinite, and the highest depends upon a combination of scholarship, sympathy, imagination, and enthusiasm in all concerned which not every group will possess, but which, when they are present, make this the finest of all methods of academic work.

(The success of an honors seminar depends upon careful reading or laboratory work, a large part of which all the members have done in common.) In addition each member will have made a more thorough study of a particular topic in the preparation of his paper. This he may present so attractively that other members of the group will make note of his references and follow up many of his points by reading for themselves. The role of the professor is to direct the discussion, to avoid lecturing, indeed to say as little as possible himself except at those points where his comment may be needed, when, the ground being duly prepared, what he does say will have a far greater effect than in any class or lecture. (The advantage of the seminar method over the individual tutorial lies precisely in this discussion.)

(The supreme model for the conduct of honors seminars is Plato's Dialogues.) Here is the place for the Socratic method and those teachers who learn to use it with skill and sympathy and patience will be most successful. To reproduce the spirit and atmosphere of a Platonic Dialogue, should be the aim of every honors seminar. Obviously a method so free and informal and spontaneous cannot be confined within the limits of an academic timetable. No honors seminar should be terminated by the ringing of an electric bell. A whole morning or afternoon or evening must be kept free for the meeting if the discussion is not to be mutilated by being cut off at a vital moment.

Teaching of this type demands all the humanity and imagination and intellectual curiosity and ripeness of scholarship which the professor has at his command. It is preferably not a job for young instructors, but rather for the oldest and strongest members of the department. Young men of ability will learn to do it effectively if they are modest and alert, but mature scholars will find that it gives scope for all their learning and all their experience.

At Swarthmore the seminar method made possible the early practice of including in the group two professors from different but related departments. This did much to unify methods of teaching. In the beginning seminars were placed in charge of heads of departments or the older and more experienced members of the faculty. As numbers of honors students increased and younger men had to be drawn into the plan they frequently served a period of apprenticeship by attending for a term or two the seminar of an older colleague. Seminars also made possible the effective use of visitors to the college. Invitations to lecture at Swarthmore were often accompanied by an invitation, sometimes a requirement, that the lecturer should reside for a certain period at the college, and during this time attend honors seminars in his subject.

The syllabus followed in an honors seminar should never be cut and dried, but rather fluid and flexible; its use will suggest constant changes and improvements. The one worked out and printed by Professor Blanshard for moral philosophy has always seemed to me a model.[1] It gives under each topic a series of references arranged roughly in the order of their

---

[1] *Moral Philosophy; A Program of Study for Honors Students*, Second edition, 1937. Printed for the department of philosophy of Swarthmore College.

importance. Following this comes a list of subjects for essays and of questions which the student is asked to ponder over until he can answer them to his own satisfaction. The material outlined for any topic would require weeks or months of work if it were covered exhaustively. The student must choose and must set his own limits. He is warned not on any account to try to read all the references, but rather to concentrate on those which best serve his purpose. It is suggested that he ought to do more work on those topics which seem to him of greatest interest and importance and less on others. A syllabus of this type is an orderly guide to the study of a subject. It enables the student to realize for himself when he has acquired a certain understanding of the most important problems, and it leaves him at the same time with a wholesome realization of how much more he might do if he wished to master the subject.

The method of teaching by seminar seemed to us at Swarthmore to have many advantages over the Oxford system of individual tutorials. The most important advantage is, as I have said, the opportunity for exchange of ideas and stimulation of thought in a group which is large enough to furnish some variety of experience and point of view and yet not too large for intimate informal talk. The seminar offers furthermore a certain protection to the student. In the individual tutorial, if teacher and pupil find themselves uncongenial, or if the teacher is not at his best, or is perhaps lacking in the power to deal effectively with the type of mind possessed by the pupil, the student is out of luck. With the best will in the world on both sides the relationship may not prove productive or stimulating and may fail of its best results without either party realizing exactly what is the matter. In the seminar this is less likely to happen. More minds are focused on the topic under discussion. Where one fails to make the illuminating comment another may succeed. Each learns from all the others, and it may easily happen that the professor may learn more than anyone else.

No one method of instruction, whatever its virtues, will suffice for all purposes. Professors who teach their honors students by the seminar method will still need to make use of individual tutorials for criticisms and suggestions too personal to be made in a group. They will wish also to send their students to a certain number of classes and lectures to obtain instruction and explanations that can be given most effectively and economically in this way. The basis of work of scientific students will of course still be the laboratory, and special problems may call for visits to government departments or industrial plants or summer courses or other universities or libraries; students and teachers who know what they want will find it in a thousand places and by a thousand means.

To a certain extent tutorial instruction has been a part of our American university system from the beginning, but the establishment of the course and hour system, together with the expansion of numbers at the turn of the century, displaced it temporarily. The very increase in size of our college and university student bodies which at first caused the decline of individual teaching eventually brought it back. The influx of large numbers of poorly prepared and poorly equipped students laid new and heavy burdens on English departments in the teaching of English composition, and it soon became apparent that by far the most effective method of teaching this subject was in individual conferences. Such conferences had become common practice in English departments before 1910 and a decade later were very widely used. The establishment of the preceptorial system at Princeton in 1905 and the introduction of tutorial work in the division of history, government, and economics at Harvard in 1914 lent impetus to the movement which has gradually spread to nearly all departments of instruction. A method of teaching which had always existed informally was regularized and standardized by the appointment of tutors on a large scale in many of the strongest universities and colleges.

The weaknesses inherent in the individual tutorial as compared with the seminar method have been noted above. Furthermore the common American organization of courses and examinations has kept the tutorial system from producing results commensurate with the expectations formed or the expense involved. Tutorial work has usually been an extra, supplementing the course and hour system, but not replacing it. For this reason neither students nor tutors have taken it seriously enough to produce the best results. The success of the student in securing a degree and in winning honors has in most colleges and universities depended upon his marks in his courses. He could neglect them only at his peril, while if he did his course work well he could neglect his tutor with impunity. In those few places where the success of the student depends entirely upon comprehensive examinations for which he prepares under the guidance of his tutor, the tutorial system has flourished; elsewhere it has been more or less half-hearted.

The lack of seriousness with which we have taken the tutorial system has had its effect on the position and prospects of the tutor himself. Because the work was not considered of first importance, tutoring was ordinarily assigned to young men. Older members of most faculties took only a small share in it or no share at all. If it had been the principal means of preparing students for examinations leading to their degree, the older members of the faculty would have undertaken it, and the privilege of personal contacts with eminent scholars would have been highly prized by the students. As a matter of fact individual instruction is much more appropriate for older men than for beginners. Here if anywhere the student deserves the best which the university has to offer, and here the teacher who possesses wisdom, scholarship, and experience can make his influence most deeply felt.

When young men are employed chiefly as tutors the problem of promotion always becomes difficult. Tutorial work is laborious, it requires long hours, and young men are not in a position to resist the assignment of undue amounts of work. The result is that they have little time or energy left for research. The work which they are doing does not widen and enrich their own scholarship as would the preparation of lectures or the conduct of classes. Tutorial work makes it difficult for them to develop the broad and deep scholarship which should be the basis of promotion, and they become, in consequence, uneasy and unhappy in their work. A teacher who hopes to rise in his profession will not remain a tutor.

The fault here lies not in the tutorial system as such, nor in the emphasis on research. The mistake is to overload young teachers with so many academic engagements that they cannot continue their education. These points deserve a moment's consideration.

The requirement as a basis of promotion of productive scholarship as evidenced by continuous publication of contributions to knowledge, while it may be enforced in a mechanical and wooden way when the mere number of pages of print and not quality of thought is considered, is, nevertheless, at bottom sound. Always giving out and never taking in makes a narrow, barren, and pedantic mind. Nothing so keeps up the enthusiasm and preserves the humility of a teacher as continuous scholarly activity. Knowledge which is merely derivative and not creative is not knowledge in its truest sense. The pedants of our academic system come from the uncreative minds. Of course so-called research may be pedantic or trivial or irrelevant to the main stream of knowledge, but if it is published it is open to criticism and the author may learn something from the reaction of his fellow scholars to his thesis, whether it is refuted by a sounder theory or, still more devastatingly, ignored.

On the other hand a man may constantly widen and deepen his scholarship by reading and reflection without publishing. If he is a perfectionist or a philosopher or a good talker (as many of the best teachers are) this is likely to be the case. Such men deserve promotion just as truly as those whose long bibliographies become still longer every year. They choose, however, an adventurous course. Their real merit is known only to their intimate associates and not always to them. Their promotion will always be slower and if they do not get their deserts in their own institution it is only by a miracle that they will find promotion elsewhere, whereas the man who publishes the results of his studies will be estimated at something like his true worth among his fellow scholars from one side of the country to the other.

The young Ph.D. is only an apprentice to scholarship. When he begins his teaching career it is the custom to expect him to do more hours of teaching than his seniors are required to undertake and he is not usually eligible for leave of absence on salary until he has been promoted to an assistant professorship. Our practice should be just the reverse. Young instructors should be given light teaching duties even if the salaries paid are reduced in proportion. They should have some opportunity to teach advanced courses, occasional leave of absence, and every possible incentive and opportunity to improve their scholarship as rapidly as possible. No college or university with which I am acquainted does its full duty by its younger teachers. An institution which did might rapidly become the training ground for the whole country by the simple process of giving young men the opportunity they need between the ages of twenty-five and thirty-five.

Individual instruction, whether by tutorials or by seminars, should be closely related to comprehensive examinations. The best students will profit by a much larger measure of freedom than would be good for those of only average ability and ambition, but this freedom is not an end in itself: it is rather a means by which they can do more and better work than would be possible if they were more narrowly restricted. Additional freedom should be matched by additional severity in the examinations for the degree. In these examinations no favors should be asked. Students trained under a freer system should be expected to come up to all the requirements set for students in the ordinary course and to do somewhat more.

The examinations for honors students are usually comprehensive, covering the work of two years in one series of tests. This is wise. Indeed, similar comprehensive examinations in the major subject for all students are rapidly becoming standard procedure all over the country, and such examinations for honors differ from those for the ordinary degree only in extent of ground covered and the more original thought expected. This adoption of comprehensive examinations marks a great improvement in American college education. Course examinations tend to become largely memory tests and, because of the limited field covered, offer too little opportunity to display ability to think, understanding of the interrelation of ideas, and grasp of the subject as a whole. Students feel instinctively that the memory is an inferior intellectual faculty and welcome even severer tests which call for putting two and two together. Of course comprehensive examinations could be made merely memory exercises on a larger scale, but to make them that would be to sacrifice their value as a measure of education.

(For comprehensive examinations the essay type is to be preferred) to the recently introduced "objective" examinations or the true-and-false type. The ability of the student to express his ideas in connected and forceful English, his skill in conveying shades of' meaning, his tact in knowing when full explanation is needed and when a brief statement of fact will suffice, his skill in contradicting views opposed to his own, his aptness in choosing illustrations are all a part of his intellectual equipment and can best be shown in examinations of the essay type.

Many advocates of the new type examinations with mechanical scoring would disagree strongly with the preceding statement. The controversy between new type examinations and those of the essay type is one which I have not space to go into here. The whole discussion is reviewed and the claims for the new type examinations stated with learning and moderation by Dr. I. L. Kandel in Bulletin 28 of the Carnegie Foundation (1936)—a monograph longer than this volume. Those who are interested in the subject are referred to Dr. Kandel's interesting and copiously annotated study. Without attempting to summarize Dr. Kandel's argument, I may content myself by emphasizing his point that no one type of examination is sufficient for all purposes. As a test of information it seems to me that the case for the new type examination is convincing. As a test of intellectual initiative, grasp of a subject, and ability to build facts and ideas into a coherent whole, which are the qualities of greatest importance in a comprehensive examination for an honors degree, it seems to me that the essay type is superior.

According to the traditional American university method,

a student is examined by the professor who has taught him. The defects of this system are obvious and where a special program of even the most limited extent is provided for abler students, the whole department frequently participates in the comprehensive examination. In a few places examiners for honors students are drawn from outside. In large universities many of the advantages of external examiners can be procured without going outside the institution. In so large a staff it is easy to find individuals who have not taught a given student, and who examine him as a stranger might. This plan is in common use and works satisfactorily, though lacking somewhat in the interest and excitement which attend the use of examiners from outside the institution.

Among the institutions inspected by the Swarthmore faculty external examiners are commonly used in only a few, among them Boston College, the University of Chattanooga, Franklin College (where, since no money can be found for the purpose in the budget, members of the faculty pay the cost out of their own pockets), Holy Cross, Kenyon, M.I.T., Mt. Holyoke, Northwestern, Park College, Reed, Rochester, Southwestern, and the University of Virginia.

Sometimes as a matter of economy a compromise is adopted between internal and external examiners. The papers are set by professors who have done the teaching, and then the answers written by the students are sent to external examiners to be read. It may be questioned whether this is worth the trouble. A more thorough plan, in which the entire conduct of the examination is entrusted to outside examiners, is much to be preferred.

The use of external examiners provides a stimulus to faculty and students alike, the value of which it would be hard to overestimate. Throughout our entire educational system in this country today there is a tendency to leave students in freedom, to do away with paltry restrictions, to give greater scope for individual initiative. This is as it should be. But it is often forgotten that increased freedom should be matched by increased responsibility. The element of stimulus and responsibility is supplied by external examiners in the most effective way possible. Such examinations are and should be an ordeal. Students dread them in advance but look back upon them afterwards with satisfaction. Despite the complete freedom in which the honors student lives and works, such an examination system will make the experience rigorous rather than soft. The tonic effect is likewise felt by members of the faculty. Under our conventional academic system it is difficult for trustees and administrative officers to obtain any kind of objective estimate of the quality of the teaching of an American college professor or even for the professor himself to estimate the effect of his work. The system of external examiners offers such an opportunity. Sincere teachers will have nothing to fear from it; they will welcome it as an opportunity to check up on themselves. But they would not be human if it did not lend an additional stimulus to their work.

Perhaps the most useful effect of external examiners, however, is the change which they make in the relationship between teacher and student. The two become allies in meeting an ordeal which is to some extent a test of both. The question which the student asks is no longer, How much are you going to require me to do? but rather, Are you sure that you are requiring enough? Easy-going professors become less popular than those who are conscientious and critical. Seminars are prolonged not because the professor is eager to keep the students, but because the students are eager to get all they can from the professor. Advice that a student should attend such-and-such lectures or do such-and-such reading is fully as effective as rules and requirements. Teaching takes on its real character when students are eager to learn, when the teacher becomes a guide rather than a taskmaster, and when the responsibility of conducting the examinations is placed upon other shoulders. Furthermore, under this plan different and sounder qualities make the teacher successful. Thorough scholarship and intellectual enthusiasm become relatively more important, and ability to popularize a subject relatively less.

Under the system of external examiners teaching in all subjects takes on something of the character of coaching athletic teams. The situations are similar. Some of the best teaching in our colleges and universities in pre-war days was done on the athletic field, not primarily because of the pedagogical skill of athletic coaches—though the best were excellent teachers—but rather because the members of the teams were eager to learn. They knew that they would have to meet in their contests a standard set not by the coach, but by their opponents, and they were anxious to be as well prepared as possible to meet that test. When the examiner in mathematics or history comes from the outside, the attitude of the students toward their professors will be found to be the same.

Examinations set and graded by external examiners can hardly be satisfactory unless arrangements are made for oral examinations in addition to the written papers. The oral should not be an additional examination covering new ground; it should be based upon the written examinations. Its purpose is to make sure in the first place that the student has properly understood the questions of the examiner and in the second place that the examiner has understood and justly appraised the answers written by the student. It gives the examiner a chance by supplementary questions to put squarely before the student the point he is asked to discuss: it gives the student a chance to amplify his reply and bring the whole range of his knowledge and thought to bear upon the point at issue. The oral examination will normally begin by a clarification of points in the student's papers of which for one reason or another the examiner wishes further discussion. Starting from there it may proceed as far as the questioner wishes in any direction. Here is the chance to probe the student's mind. A good examiner will continue to dig deeper and deeper until he strikes bottom. The experience will and should be a strenuous one for the student, but he will enjoy the recollection of it after it is over.

The true art of examining is not to attempt to find out what the student does not know, but rather to estimate how thorough is his grasp of the things he knows best. If his best is mediocre his case is not much improved if he knows fifty things up to an indifferent standard instead of forty. On the other hand, if his best is good enough, the gaps in his knowledge are not important. He can readily fill them up at any time. The basis of judgment should be qualitative rather than quantitative. This point of view is a difficult one for American professors to accept. They have been accustomed all their lives to the administration of quantitative requirements for the A.B. degree. We put our trust in averages, not realizing that they are wholly fallacious as measurements of educational realities. If a student receives a grade of 90 in physics and 70 in French the average is 80, but this figure is really meaningless. A true standard is one which professors would instinctively use in measuring the merits of a man who was a candidate for an instructorship. The question at issue would then be his capacity in the subject he is expected to teach. Mastery of other fields of knowledge would constitute valuable additional qualifications, while ignorance of anything outside his own subject would be a serious handicap.

The basis of choice would not be quantitative, but rather qualitative—an appraisal which, while too vague to be expressed in figures, would not be difficult to arrive at in practice and would be much more accurate as a basis for making the appointment. External examiners will reach more accurate and juster results if they think of the students before them as candidates for some kind of an appointment rather than as competitors in some kind of game of artificial numerical averages.

Examinations of the type I have been discussing are of course tests of ability as well as of attainment. That they should be. Their one great practical value is their accuracy as a prediction of success in after life in which ability counts for much though not for everything.

No good examination can be mechanical. The best examiners are men and women who have sympathy, imagination, intuition, and human wisdom as well as courageous and vigorous scholarship. Such individuals are rare, but an educational program worthy of the small group of our best undergraduates cannot be operated by teachers and examiners of mediocre ability. External examiners of the highest type make a great contribution to the education of the students whom they examine and to the members of the faculty whose charges are being tested.[2]

[2] An excellent account of the experience of Swarthmore College with outside examiners is Robert E. Spiller, "Ten Years of Outside Examiners," *English Journal* (College Edition), V. 22, pp. 310-319. April, 1933.

CHAPTER TEN

ADMINISTRATIVE AND FINANCIAL PROBLEMS

IN THE inauguration of a new plan of academic work such as the one here discussed educational machinery and administrative devices can make a real contribution to success, or, if badly chosen, can make success difficult. A study of the way in which plans work in different places shows how important is the role of the president or the academic dean in the inauguration of new methods. Members of the faculty, however wise and enthusiastic, can make small headway without administrative support. The reverse is also true: it is practically impossible for an administrative officer to coerce an unwilling faculty in an enterprise where so much depends on enthusiasm and morale. Among the institutions which have been unsuccessful with work of this type it would be difficult to say whether more plans are working badly because of opposition from the faculty or from the administration. Either is fatal and unity is a first requisite.

Some plans have been wrecked by administrative impatience and some by administrative indifference. When a college president, too much in a hurry, attempts to start honors work full scale with too little preliminary discussion the result is certain to be failure. This has been the case in a number of institutions. Where the plan has received a black eye for such reasons, it is more difficult to revive it than it was to make the first beginning. On the other hand some plans drag along very slowly because of administrative indifference. Without whole-hearted co-operation from the administration even an enthusiastic faculty can accomplish little. Administrative adjustments as to hours and schedule will be needed; the plan must be defended against its critics. The application of more rigorous standards will at first antagonize some students and alarm some parents, and any change in any college or university will always be resented by some of its alumni. The president is the person to whom sooner or later complaints and objections are bound to come and he is the logical person to reply. The answering of such critics is good fun for the man who enjoys that kind of thing, and the man who does not had better not be a college president.

The first rule of educational wisdom in inaugurating a new plan of study is to begin slowly. The introduction of any new educational device on too large a scale is a precarious enterprise. If a beginning is made with small numbers, if growth is slow and prudent, the problems which arise can be solved by discussion and experiment without confusion. Rules can be altered and adjustments made wherever necessary, and experience gained which will be invaluable in the application of new methods to larger groups.

During twenty years of experience with honors work at Swarthmore probably most of the difficulties which such a plan would face anywhere were encountered and overcome— all, that is, except three. We never had at Swarthmore to contend with the handicap of that type of academic conservatism which refuses open-minded consideration of new proposals merely because they are new, and refuses change because it is change. Nor were we, in the second place, faced with the problem of overwhelming numbers with which only the methods of mass education can cope. Nor had we, in the third place, to contend with the difficulties which faculties make for themselves by trying to do several things at once, maintaining several different plans of independent study at the same time, and offering a bewildering variety of commencement honors based upon different and often contradictory principles. Our plan was simple; we placed all our eggs in one basket and concentrated all the resources of the College on the task of making a success of the program we had chosen.

That task was simple but it was not easy. We had to meet the usual objections and opposition from students, from their parents, and from alumni. We had the usual competition between academic work and athletics and extra-curricular activities. Some of the good features of the College, such as the lively academic competition between fraternities based upon the publication each semester of fraternity averages, proved to be inconsistent with honors work. Honors students had no averages; if the best members of a fraternity withdrew in order to read for honors the prestige of the group suffered. When it came to a conflict between fraternity loyalty and the opportunity for a better education by the new plan, fraternity loyalty would always prevail. Consequently this competition had to be dropped although it had proved a useful means of enlisting the efforts of upperclassmen and alumni to make sure that even the mediocre members of each group did the best work of which they were capable. We had finally the usual discussion of the bearing of special facilities for superior students upon the concept of democracy, and the usual financial problems.

All these difficulties are real. They look easy only after they have been overcome. As they arise they mean sleepless nights, uncomfortable interviews, the loss of gifts and legacies, and the threatened wreck of plans on the success of which men and women are staking their academic future. Nor is it always the central and most fundamental objections that are hardest to meet. There will be in every college or university a thousand minor difficulties: small, unimportant, harmless customs and traditions, inextricably woven into the conventional course-and-hour system, which conflict with the new plan, cause friction, and prevent the smooth running of the machine. A certain popular lecture course has long been a tradition of the college, but no longer will honors students be required to attend lectures. The graduates of a certain school have for ten years maintained a "two-point" average, but for the best students averages are now to be abolished. A prize is offered for the best student in the Junior class, but the best Juniors no longer have any kind of academic record on the basis of which the prize can be given. The lacrosse team has for several years made a fine showing, but like a bolt from the blue the stunned alumni hear that the captain has decided not to play in the spring of his Senior year in order that he may have more time to prepare for his honors examinations. The nervous parents of a brilliant girl forbid her to read for honors because they fear that the concentration involved may be injurious to her health. They might fear similar injury from too much social life, but it would never occur to them to forbid her to attend the parties to which she had been invited.

Such difficulties and objections, large and small, in some institutions have prevented the adoption of an honors plan and in others have limited the plans adopted to a few tentative steps. Timid faculties tend to make the whole process too complicated, to tie up themselves and their students by too many rules and regulations, to provide against imaginary difficulties which in practice arise only once in a hundred times, to cross bridges before they get to them, and to break butterflies on wheels.

The most persistent objection to this breaking of the academic lock step, to giving abler students harder work, is our academic interpretation or misinterpretation of the idea of democracy. If all men are born free and equal why should some be given a better education than others? The word "better" begs the question. The best education for any individual is that which will develop his powers to the utmost and best fit him to realize his own ideal of the good life. The world would be a dull place if all men and women were alike. Ability to deal with the abstract subjects of a university course is only one kind of ability. There are many others equally valuable both for individual happiness and for service to society. Some kinds of ability cannot be advantageously developed in a college or university, but may thrive best in the art school, or the workshop, or in practical life. Some students can get something from a college course but cannot use all that the college is prepared to teach. For some men a little mathematics or philosophy will go a long way and the upper levels of these subjects will prove not helpful but merely bewildering. Some students can advance a considerable way if they are allowed to go slowly, with careful explanation at every step, and constant drill and review. Others work best at a faster pace and will go much further, even as far as the frontiers of knowledge, before their curiosity is satisfied.

It is a travesty on democracy to maintain that all these undergraduates should be taught the same subjects, at the same rate of speed, by the same methods. Yet that, if one may judge from their actions, is what the members of certain college faculties appear to believe. If pressed they would probably say that the university does not exist to serve all levels of ability and that due account of differences is taken by grades which range from A to D, or from 60 to 100 per cent. The answer is that American colleges and universities have thrown open their doors to students of the widest range of ability and interests and those doors are not likely to be closed. I for one would strongly oppose closing them. The range of ability to master any given branch of knowledge represented, even in the most carefully chosen student body, is very much wider than our grading system: instead of the ratio of 60 to 100, we have ratios of one to five or one to ten or possibly one to a hundred. The differences are so great as to become qualitative and defy quantitative measurement.

Even our most conservative faculties tend to recognize these differences more easily when it comes to a question of special help for students below the average who cannot keep up with their classes. The same professors who are glad to see special help provided for weaker students will take the line that the best students can look after themselves. What if they are bored occasionally in class listening to slow and stumbling replies to questions to which they already know the answers? What if they are required to do unnecessary exercises and submit to drill they do not need? All this will do them no serious harm and once they have finished the A.B. and the Ph.D. they can go their own gait.

This is, of course, to a certain extent true. The worst educational system will not ruin all the good students. It will, however, injure many by discouraging them with intellectual pursuits, by teaching them habits of idleness, by denying them the kind of growth which comes only with the exertion of all of their powers, by giving them an exaggerated idea of their own merits, and by sheer waste of their time. Modern life is complex; the conditions of success in any intellectual pursuit are exacting; for it the highest excellence which can be reached by our educational system will be none too good. Democracy needs the best young men and women trained to the height of their powers, if we are to solve the problems which confront us in industry, in science, in the professions, and in public life. Democracy needs these young people trained in habits of industry; it needs that they should develop all their initiative and independence, their courage and perseverance in attacking difficult problems; that they should preserve their humility by the habit of comparing themselves with others of like powers. It is good that weaker students should be helped to make the most of themselves, but what happens to the best makes much more difference to the welfare of society than what happens to the poorest.

Students who desire by taking extra courses to graduate in three years will often find the program of independent work impossible. They must choose between speed and quality, and too often they choose speed. Similarly students who are working their way through college may find it impossible to give the extra time needed for independent study. Where the academic curriculum is standardized and regimented, students who have sufficient energy and ability may often get a better education than they otherwise would because of the necessity of earning money. They learn from the work they do as well as from their studies. But when studies become sufficiently interesting and important the situation changes for those who possess real intellectual interests, and such students would go further if they could be supported on scholarship funds instead of having to earn money for their living and their tuition fees. What is good for the practical man who will make his career in business or some kind of administrative work may not be best for the student who has a genuine vocation for the intellectual life.

Another difficulty arises from current misconception of the idea of breadth in education. Programs specifically organized to give abler students a better mastery of their particular field of interest usually involve more work in the major, or a focus on two or three related subjects; as for example, economics, political science, and history; or physics, mathematics, and chemistry. The cross-fertilization of ideas which is made possible by advanced work in two or three connected subjects is extremely illuminating, and a well-planned course of this type has much more educational value than the usual more or less haphazard selection of courses. But it runs counter to many cherished American ideas of education. The typical undergraduate is likely to have a strong desire for what he thinks of as breadth, by which he means taking elementary courses in every subject which has even mildly attracted his curiosity. Under the free elective system, the typical student, left to himself, will spend about half the time of his four years in taking elementary courses. This is unfortunate. The essence of education is not acquiring information but learning to think. It is impossible to think until one has acquired a certain store of facts and ideas: the purpose of the elementary course is normally to supply these materials for thought which advanced courses offer opportunities to use. Most students would get a better education if they restricted their range, took fewer subjects, and did more advanced work in those selected, leaving their curiosity about some departments of knowledge to be satisfied by outside reading in later life.

It is not merely the student's preference for smatterings of many subjects over mastery of a few that stands in the way of a more closely organized and organically related undergraduate program. The requirements of the various professional schools are likely in practice to have the same effect, as does also the prescription by state boards of a certain number of hours of work in education as a prerequisite for a license to teach. The professional schools, especially those of law and medicine, will usually be found willing to waive part of their prescribed program for undergraduates and to admit those who seem to be best educated, but requirements in education for teachers' licenses are strictly enforced.

These required "hours" of education are a poor substitute for postgraduate professional training. It would be hard to prove that a few courses in education (which are often mediocre in themselves and which are supplied in many places by none-too-creditable subterfuges) add much to the effectiveness of the young teacher's work, while it is certain that sounder and more thorough training in his specialty would do so. It is not sufficient that a young teacher be a few steps ahead of the class so far as subject matter is concerned. A well-trained mathematician will teach elementary arithmetic or algebra in a way which is impossible for the teacher who has himself explored only the elements of the subject. In this respect, as in so many others, devices intended to ameliorate the defects of a bad educational system stand in the way of making that system over into a better one. Difficulties of the kind I have been enumerating may seem slight and unimportant, but in practice they are like sand in the gears and may slow down the operation of a new and better organization of college and university studies.

More sand is thrown into the gears by the elaborate organization of athletics and extra-curricular activities, in which undergraduates find an outlet for energy and initiative for which the conventional course system offers too little scope. These activities are not merely play; they are a part of the serious business of college life. Many college graduates will say that they got the best part of their education outside the classroom, and while that may sometimes be an exaggeration, the sad fact is that too often it is true. The extent and variety of these outside activities are the marvel of every foreign observer of our colleges and universities. The honors thus won are taken very seriously by the undergraduates, are carefully recorded in yearbooks and annuals, and are scrutinized by employment managers whose business it is to select college graduates for jobs.

Moderate participation in extra-curricular activities is salutary and wholesome, but the theory held by most undergraduates, that the more clubs and societies and teams and publications a man may take part in the better, is an illusion. The law of diminishing returns begins to operate as the number of such distractions increases. Frequently in our large universities these activities themselves (for example, managerships of athletic teams) become so standardized as to exclude the opportunity for individual initiative which ought to be their justification, and become merely drudgery. At the best these activities are haphazard. They offer only a fraction of the educational value commonly attributed to them. They are supposed to be training in leadership, but too often they make it impossible for the student to lay the groundwork of education upon which any real leadership in the modern world must be based. Rhodes Scholarship Committees of Selection, which take into account "instincts for leadership" as one of the elements upon which appointments are based, have had to be warned against excessive participation in extra-curricular activities for precisely this reason. The review of the life histories of the members of the Harvard class of 1911, twenty-five years after graduation, offers striking evidence of the unreliability of success in undergraduate teams, clubs, and societies as a prediction of success in after life.

Any academic program which enlists strongly the interest of the abler students, which offers them freedom and independence, and which demands of them the best they can do, will inevitably conflict with the traditional addiction to social and athletic activities. If the academic program offers better scope for the qualities of initiative and independence, as it should, and if it is tested by examinations which compare in severity and ruthlessness with the tests of athletic prowess, studies will win out in the end. The instinct of the students will be found to be sound at bottom. They are eager for the best education they can get; their failure to take the course and hour system any more seriously than they do is justified, though they may not think out clearly the reasons for their attitude, and the best of them will in the end give to a better program the effort and devotion it deserves.

The revolution in undergraduate attitude involved is startling to alumni—even to some professors. To have varsity football players cutting practice to finish a laboratory test, to have men refusing the presidency of this society or that because of the fact that the duties would interfere with their work, to have students refusing to go home for a vacation in order to have quiet time to catch up on some particularly laborious reading, or to work on a paper in which they are especially interested—all these are new phenomena in undergraduate life, and they will at first excite unfavorable comment. Parents will be alarmed and some members of the alumni body outraged. Well-meaning but educationally naive national officers of fraternities will shake their heads and fear the worst. There will be tempests in various teapots. But if the faculty proceeds steadily on its way the native shrewdness and sense of proportion of the students may be trusted to meet all these petty obstacles and in one or two decades convert all but a few die-hards to whole-hearted support of the new plan.

(The expense of individual instruction and supervision is an administrative consideration which checks the development of honors work in many colleges and universities. This is a real difficulty which cannot be ignored.) Enthusiastic professors will often undertake the supervision of honors work as an extra and this is not an impossible way of beginning. It may be doubted, however, whether it is feasible in the long run. Eventually everyone concerned will tire of the extra burden and the new program will gradually be abandoned. Any institution which aspires to develop a healthy and growing program of honors study must make allowance in the teaching load of the professors concerned for the time spent in tutorial or seminar work.

This can often be done by limiting the number of regular courses. Almost every American college and university offers too many. The variety of the educational menu presented is bewildering to students in large universities and an intolerable burden upon the faculties of small colleges. A leaner and more closely knit program would be better for all concerned. That institution is rare which could not free enough teaching time by this means to provide for a modest honors program. But as the program develops additional instruction will have to be provided.

For an honors program embracing one-fourth to one-third of the members of the Junior and Senior classes, the additional cost of instruction will amount to fifteen or twenty per cent. Some saving will result from the fact that students who are working independently under tutorial guidance need not be cared for in ordinary advanced classes. The problem, however, is not merely quantitative. Mediocre teachers will not make a success of honors work and improving the quality of the teaching staff will entail additional expense. Individual instruction is more exacting than the conduct of classes. It is not sufficient that the instructor prepare a certain topic or, perhaps using old notes, be ready to deliver a lecture on a given subject. The discussion in tutorial or seminar will range far and wide and will test the professor's grasp of the whole subject. Furthermore, personal qualities are much more important in close relations with undergraduates—intellectual honesty, flexibility, tolerance, skill in conducting discussion, freedom from pedantry, sound scholarship as distinct from the showmanship which may enable a superficial scholar to "get by" in dealing with a larger class.

During a period of twenty years in which honors work has been given at Swarthmore to a constantly increasing number of students the budget for salaries has been increased from $100,000 to $300,000 with a comparatively small increase (from 500 to 700) in the total number of students. This increased expense has been mainly not for an increased amount of teaching but rather for improved quality. The faculty has grown in size but still more in excellence, and the greatest expense has been for higher salaries rather than for more instructors and professors. It cannot be too strongly emphasized that work for superior students cannot be successfully directed by mediocre teachers.

In addition to the cost of instruction a certain minimum equipment of libraries and laboratories is indispensable. For independent study textbooks will not suffice. The increased demand which honors work makes on library facilities is noted elsewhere. At Swarthmore in twenty years the library budget was increased by about $45,000 per year and the number of books by about 85,000. Comparable demands will be made by honors students in science on laboratory facilities.[1]

The whole subject of the needs and functions of college libraries has been admirably treated by Professor Harvie Branscomb. While he could find no statistics reflecting the demand of honors students on library facilities, his general impression agrees with the statements made above. It is safe to say that the library budget which he suggests as desirable will be found to be the minimum for a college which wishes to provide adequate facilities for its most ambitious students. Mr. Edward B. Stanford, who has studied the specific problem of the demand of honors work on college libraries, likewise emphasizes the increased demand of honors students both for books and for library service. In spite of the lack of pertinent statistics he concludes that "all available evidence points to an increased use (whether recorded or not) of printed materials in every institution with a strong and successful program of independent study."[2]

There is another item of expense which must be taken into account by any administration which hopes to make a success of a long-range honors program. Individual teaching is absorbing. The best instructors will give prodigally of their time and strength in fostering the development of eager and ambitious students. Such work is likely to leave them very little of the uninterrupted leisure needed for their own

[1] The reports of Comptroller N. O. Pittenger and Librarian Charles B. Shaw of Swarthmore, attached to the President's report for 1939 (*Bulletin of Swarthmore College* XXXVII, 3, Fourth Month, 1940, pp. 33 ff. and 69 ff.), review the expenditure of the College for the period 1921-39, both for instruction and for the library. These expenditures are not merely given as totals but also analyzed in the form of dollars per student.

[2] Harvie Branscomb, *Teaching with Books*, published jointly by the Association of American Colleges and American Library Association, 1940. Edward B. Stanford, "Honors Work and the College Library," *Library Quarterly*, V, XII, 2. April, 1942.

scholarly work. Some men can combine the two, but many of the best cannot. These individuals must be protected from their own generosity, not merely for their own sakes but also for the sake of the work they are doing. The best students learn most from productive scholars. Unless the teacher is also growing, his pupils will cease to grow. The ideal way of ensuring the development of the unselfish teacher is by the provision of frequent and generous leaves of absence. These periods of leave should not be considered as vacations for rest or recreation, as sabbaticals so often are. They should be for research and should be granted on somewhat the same terms as research fellowships, on the basis of a definite plan of work, the results of which will be scrutinized at the end of the period of leave. Summer vacations provide all the time that any teacher reasonably needs for rest and refreshment. The man who is not interested in advancing his own scholarship may as well teach through his lifetime without leave of absence. Indeed the summer vacation is more than a healthy man should need for rest, and the advancement of young scholars may be a direct result of effective use of the long vacation for study and research.

Professors and administrative officers in one institution know too little about what is happening in others, and more frequent visits, made with a definite purpose for the observation of work and the study of laboratory and library facilities, would help almost any faculty to improve the conduct of its work. Educational and scholarly associations do not meet this need. What is wanted is observation on the spot, during term time. Professors will learn much both as to what to do and what not to do. It is not advisable that our educational institutions should seek to develop standardized procedure to be followed everywhere. There is enough variety in good ideas to enable every college or university to develop its own character and atmosphere, but those institutions are likely to be most individual which know most about what is being done elsewhere.

The impulse to look abroad, to study what is being done in other places, must usually come from the administration. Faculties fall easily into ruts and come to accept their own methods and traditions as inevitable. They will as a rule be shaken out of their complacency only by wide-awake presidents and deans. It is not sufficient, however, that presidents and deans do the visiting. Members of the faculty must themselves see what other faculties are doing, if the institution is to get the best results, by way of either warning or example. Central national control of a system of higher education as broad and varied as ours would be an unmitigated calamity. National self-consciousness, however, on the part of those who are responsible for the teaching in our universities and colleges would be an unmixed blessing.

Work of the character described in this book is not for all institutions. During the last twenty years the movement has spread rapidly in the United States, perhaps too rapidly. Upon administrative officers mainly rests the responsibility of determining whether a given college or university should or should not undertake it. But it is inevitable that in many cases heads of weak institutions should be more ambitious than their resources justify, while heads of strong institutions are too prone to rest content with their traditional program. In the long run, however, these problems will settle themselves; insecurely based plans will fail, while too conservative colleges and universities will be forced by more progressive rivals to move forward with the procession. Meanwhile administrative wisdom and good sense will save much lost motion and enable a given college or university to find the kind of work it can do best. It has been said that no individual ever made a success who did not estimate accurately his own strength and weaknesses and no one ever made a failure who did. The same principle applies to a college or a university.

Chapter Eleven

THE FRESHMAN AND SOPHOMORE YEARS

⸨During his first two years the American college student is largely occupied with work of secondary-school character, completing his preparation to meet university standards.⸩ He usually needs training in English composition and in thoughtful reading of English literature. Practically always he needs work in foreign languages to satisfy even the modest requirements which are the rule in American colleges.⸨Perhaps nothing would improve the quality of American education more than such a shift in high-school work and in the first two years of college as to give the student by the beginning of his Junior year an easy reading knowledge of two languages besides his own.⸩This requirement is at present enforced only with difficulty for postgraduate work. The student must, furthermore, in the first two years of college, satisfy the distribution requirements of his university and take elementary courses in the two or three subjects in which he expects to do advanced work in his Junior and Senior years.

Many interesting experiments are being made with the purpose of eliminating lost motion in these first two years, saving students from confusion and floundering, and bringing them up to the Junior year better prepared for the tasks of the upper division. Preliminary periods for orientation and placement are often arranged for Freshmen before college opens. The responsibility of advising Freshmen in the planning of their course as a whole is taken much more seriously today than it was a few years ago. It is common to assign Freshmen and their parents pertinent reading some months in advance to guide them in solving the all-important problem of the choice of courses in college.

The revolutionary plan for the lower division in operation at the University of Chicago has already been described, as well as the facilities provided for high-ranking students during the first two years at Boston College, Holy Cross, Mt. Holyoke, and Princeton. Other notable attempts to improve the opportunity open to beginning students are being made at Yale and Stanford. At Yale the work of the first year is in charge of a special group of professors and administrative officers. The programs of the schools from which the students come are carefully studied, and before the opening of college the deans have accumulated a substantial amount of information about the tastes and aptitudes of each student. The Freshmen are given a well-written and informative booklet on the subject of choosing courses at Yale, and on the basis of information contained in the booklet, Freshmen are expected to submit a tentative plan of work as early as the beginning of August preceding their entrance in September.

The Yale program is noteworthy because of the fact that special facilities are offered to Freshmen whose ability and preparation are better than the average. Freshman classes are sectioned on the basis of ability and the work done in the better sections is expected to be much greater in amount and higher in quality than would be possible for the average. Students who are prepared to do so are encouraged to enroll in advanced courses, and more than one-third avail themselves of this privilege. Instead of being disheartened, as the better Freshmen often are, by the regimentation which is so common in the first two years, entering students at Yale are from the beginning given the opportunity to do the best work of which they are capable. They are relieved from the monotony of going over again subjects which they have already covered in preparatory school, and are kept stretching, which is the secret of educational advancement.

Sectioning classes on the basis of ability is perhaps the most feasible method of making the work of the first two years mean most to the best students. The usual practice has been to herd all levels of ability and interest together into large groups and to submit them to a common, rigid, strictly regimented series of requirements which are invariably too easy for the best and too hard for the poorest. A certain uniformity of subject matter is inevitable in these two preparatory years —English, foreign languages, distribution requirements, and elementary courses in the field in which the student expects to do advanced work in his last two years. But it makes all the difference in the world how thoroughly these elementary subjects are mastered. The mass of the students can achieve only a modest standard. The best, if they are segregated, can achieve results which professors, wearied by years of standardized routine, behold only in their dreams and never expect to see realized.

Aside from the custom of sectioning elementary classes on the basis of ability, which is gradually becoming more common, little attempt has been made in American colleges and universities to provide a special program for students of superior ability in the period of the first two years. As a rule all are treated alike and on the basis of the showing made in the elementary courses during these two years the superior students are admitted to honors work at the beginning of the Junior year.

A more ambitious attempt to meet the needs of the superior students during the first two years is the system of independent study in the lower division at Stanford. This work has already been briefly described. So far as numbers go it is easily the most important part of the Stanford plan, and the members of the Stanford faculty are strongly convinced of its importance. "The student who needs independent study most of all," says Professor Robinson in the report already cited, "and who profits most as a general rule is the Freshman." The report makes the points that the Freshman enters the university at a critical stage in his own development when individual guidance may mean more to him than at any later stage of his career, and that independent work and individual instruction are even more necessary for leading him to understand the importance of laying the foundation for a broad liberal education in his first two years than for the relatively more specialized work of the upper division. The Stanford faculty believes that the result of setting free the abler Freshmen and Sophomores to pursue harder and more independent work is to raise the level of the work done by all students in the lower division and to propagate throughout the whole community a broader conception of education. These arguments carry great weight, coming as they do from the institution which has had so much experience with independent study for underclassmen.

Sectioning elementary classes on the basis of ability during the first two years of college greatly improves the preparation of superior students for advanced work. If to this are added facilities for independent study in connection with courses, as at Stanford, the opportunities for abler students are still further improved. There is reason to expect that certain other universities will eventually inaugurate something like the Chicago plan, substituting for these expedients a completely independent program in the Freshman and Sophomore years. It would only be necessary to establish comprehensive examinations for admission to the Junior class something like those now required at Chicago and Goucher and allow the best students to prepare for these examinations under tutorial guidance, making use of regular classes to whatever extent they might find desirable, without placing upon the student any responsibility for course examinations and without giving him any course credit. The intermediate comprehensive examination would in this case probably take several different forms which would qualify those who were successful for admission to various honors courses in the Junior year. It would doubtless be advisable to insist upon a certain number of common subjects—for example English and foreign languages. There would be in addition papers in certain subjects specified as prerequisite for honors work in various fields. Over and above these, papers would be set to ensure a certain measure of distribution—papers in the humanities and social studies for scientific students and papers in science for students whose principal interest lay in literary fields. Admission to honors work in the upper years would of course depend upon the quality of the student's work in this intermediate examination.

Under so free a system the amount of time spent in preparation for this examination might likewise be flexible as it is at Chicago. Able students who had enjoyed exceptional advantages in secondary school might be ready for it in one year; students who found that they had more ground to cover, or who perhaps were not sure of their plans and decided at the last moment to change from one field to another, or who were ambitious to acquire an exceptionally broad preparation, might be allowed to spend three years. The rigid time schedule of the American college course, the importance which our students and their parents attach to its completion in four years, to "graduating with their class," constitutes in itself a kind of regimentation. There are the best of reasons why the time spent in preparation for the A.B. degree should be only three years in some cases and as much as five in others. For social purposes class organization could quite as well be based upon the year in which a student entered college (as is the case in England) rather than upon the year in which he completed his course.

No American college or university except Chicago has as yet adopted so free a program for the first two years as I have sketched in the preceding paragraphs. There are certain practical difficulties. The quality of the preparation of the students in secondary schools varies between wide limits. High-school records are not an adequate basis for the selection of the ablest students, and even though permission to try independent work were granted liberally to all of those interested, there would inevitably be many instances where the fit were excluded and the unfit given tasks beyond their powers. Some of the best students enter college with the poorest preparation. Most Freshmen are as yet unfamiliar with the method of independent study while they do understand the course and hour system. This situation will change as secondary schools adopt more generally the plan of giving a better training to those able to profit by it. For all these reasons the difficulties of such a plan for the first two years may be temporary rather than permanent, and the time may be approaching when colleges and universities generally will not fear to extend the freedom of the honors method to the Freshman and Sophomore years.

CHAPTER TWELVE

HONORS WORK IN SECONDARY SCHOOLS

FORTY years ago President Eliot had his attention called to the fact that a certain small private school in Louisville was sending boys to Harvard unusually well prepared for college work. The principal of this school was a young graduate of Johns Hopkins by the name of Abraham Flexner.

In response to an inquiry from President Eliot as to the secret of his success with boys, Mr. Flexner explained his methods. He was not a hard taskmaster and he made little use of the classroom drill which was supposed to be the best means of preparing boys to pass college entrance examinations. Instead he allowed his pupils a great degree of freedom. It was his custom to promise a boy whom he admitted to the school that he would without fail secure his admission to Harvard or to any other college. Mr. Flexner made no promises, however, as to the length of time this preparation might take. That depended upon the boy. If he did not work hard it would take longer; if he did his best the time would be shorter; and if in addition to working hard he happened to be a boy of superior ability the time would be shorter still. The response of his pupils to this challenge to their initiative made Abraham Flexner's reputation as a schoolmaster. He was using methods, rare in those days, which are now beginning to be adopted by high schools and preparatory schools all over the country—methods which break the lock step of the rigid curriculum and give to pupils of varying interests and capacities the opportunity which each needs most.

The study made in this chapter of this vast pioneering effort is perforce inadequate, but it may be hoped that it will serve to illustrate the great changes now taking place and call the reader's attention to their importance. The number of secondary schools in the country is so large that within the limited time available the members of the Swarthmore faculty have been able to inspect only a small fraction of the total number —indeed by no means all of the schools which habitually send graduates to Swarthmore.

This chapter is based partly on such inspections as could be made, partly upon material already available in printed form assembled largely by means of questionnaires. Information of this kind is in the nature of things unsatisfactory in dealing with unstandardized methods of teaching and study. It is unsatisfactory, furthermore, because the conditions under which high schools and private preparatory schools do their work vary widely in different parts of the country, as do the standards of achievement which can be enforced. A survey of secondary-school facilities for superior pupils covering the entire country and based upon first-hand visits of inspection would be a formidable task but if well done it would yield results of the greatest value and importance. It is evident that the last two decades have witnessed an immense amount of pioneer work on this problem, and that we are here dealing with what is perhaps the greatest step forward that has been taken in secondary education since the inauguration of uniform entrance requirements brought some kind of order out of the confusion of secondary-school work in the 1890's. The adoption of a system of units and the examinations set by the College Entrance Examination Board produced a uniformity of standards much needed at the time. The common measuring rod thus provided is still useful, but the regimentation which was a by-product of these reforms has now served its purpose. Conditions have changed. Numbers have increased. Schools are called upon to serve many other purposes besides preparing students for college, and they must deal with pupils of a much wider range of ability. If the schools are to meet successfully the needs of pupils of this great range of interests and abilities, they must work out for themselves new methods, and it is evident that this is what they are at present all over the country endeavoring to do.

Important as it is to provide special facilities for superior students in our colleges and universities, it is still more important to do this in the schools. The effects of regimentation, which are so harmful in our colleges, are even more disastrous to younger students in the secondary and elementary years. The facts about the number of students enrolled would lead one to expect *a priori* the presence in our school system of students of the widest possible range of ability and aptitude, and the experience of school men indicates that this is true. About fifteen per cent of our boys and girls of college age actually go to college; four times that many, or sixty per cent of those of high-school age are enrolled in public high schools or private preparatory schools. It is obvious that the range of ability must extend from the highest to the lowest, and that no single curriculum and no common standard of achievement can possibly meet the needs of so heterogeneous a group.

Under any system of regimentation standards are inevitably lowered to suit the ability of the majority. The poorest fail and the best students do not receive the stimulus they need to do their best work and to develop their powers to the fullest extent. Democracy pays a fearful price in terms of trained leadership for this failure to make the most of our best brains. A research bulletin of the National Education Association dealing with this subject quotes an admirable statement on this point from the White House Conference on Child Health and Protection held in 1931:

It is agreed that in a democracy more than in any other form of government, high-grade leadership is essential. The United States of America with its Congress; with its forty-eight commonwealths, each with its legislature; with its hundreds of municipalities, each with its own local government; must have intelligent leaders or fail in the struggle. Surely there was never greater need of able leadership than at the present time. And yet there are *one million and a half* children in our public schools with exceptionally good brains and exceptionally high intelligence, who need only the permission and the opportunity to develop the leadership for which they have the foundation; therefore, we urge that the White House Conference and all intelligent, patriotic citizens of the United States take active and efficient steps to save this large number of children from the idleness, the more or less malicious mischief and the neglect which is their portion in the average public schools of today. Aside from the injustice to the child himself, it is almost a social crime to neglect these highly endowed children.[1]

Certainly the school authorities of the country are fully alive to the importance of this problem. It is the subject of a large and growing literature, and an immense amount of admirable experimental work is already being done. About few schools could the statement be made that results as yet are fully satisfactory, but they are highly promising. Twenty years ago the common and, indeed, the sole procedure for dealing with unusually bright students was to allow them to advance more rapidly from grade to grade, and to graduate from one to three years younger than the average. This method was open to the obvious objection that children so treated found themselves under the necessity of making all

[1] NEA *Research Bulletin.* Vol. XIX, No. 4, Sept. 1941.

the adjustments necessary in association with companions from one to three years older than themselves. Today the weight of opinion of the teaching profession seems to be opposed to this plan and in favor of giving brighter pupils harder and more advanced work, keeping them in school for the regulation time, but allowing them the opportunity to acquire a better education. It would seem clear that this is the sounder plan. There is no advantage, indeed there may be a serious disadvantage, in having bright pupils graduate from high school at sixteen instead of eighteen, but there would be everything to gain in having them at eighteen two years further advanced in their work than they are on the average at present.

The experience of many European countries shows that this result can be attained. In no country in Europe does so large a proportion of the population receive the benefits of secondary education as in the United States. But in the leading countries boys and girls who do attend secondary schools will at the age of eighteen be about two years further advanced than American students of the same age. This difference is not due to any difference of ability between the best American and the best European students, but rather to the fact that in Europe the less gifted students are not admitted to the secondary schools, while in this country they are not only admitted but are allowed to set the pace.

If those high-school students who rank in the upper third in ability were allowed to go their own gait, it seems clear that, given adequate teaching, they might easily do in high school at least the equivalent of the Freshman year of college, perhaps more, and this without working any harder on their studies than they do at present, with just as much time as they now have for play. The whole difference would be made by saving the time they now waste waiting for their slower comrades to catch up. All this would involve laying no unreasonable burdens upon childish shoulders. They would do their work just as easily as they do at present and enjoy it more.

A good picture of the strides which have been made toward this goal in our public high schools is given in a research bulletin published by the National Education Association in September, 1941, "High School Methods with Superior Students." The report is based upon a questionnaire sent to 5000 high-school principals, of whom more than 1000 replied. The procedure in these 1000 schools is admirably digested and the bulletin contains as well a useful bibliography covering various aspects of the problem. It is not my purpose here to attempt a full summary of the material of the bulletin, but only to emphasize certain points which it makes.

The report discusses in some detail the definition of mentally superior children and comments upon the various tests and other criteria now in use in the schools for their identification, including the vexed question of the constancy of the I.Q. and the improvability of intelligence in a favorable environment. It gives an admirable summary of the mental and personal characteristics of superior children. Contrary to the prevailing idea, they are on the average stronger and healthier than ordinary children, are fond of games, less inclined to nervous disorders, seldom unsocial though they tend naturally to associate with others of similar mental age, and they rank above the average of unselected children in respect to moral qualities. They tend naturally to become leaders among their classmates and are likely to be chosen by their fellow pupils for positions of responsibility except in the case of very unusual children—ugly ducklings with I.Q.'s above 170—who are likely to be so far beyond the average group in their ways of thinking as to be misunderstood and distrusted by them.

Exceptional children not merely do all kinds of school work more rapidly than the average, but are furthermore capable of doing work of a different character, in which logical thinking, the recognition of obscure relationships, and the need for drawing conclusions from available data are more important than memory for facts. They are not so superior in spelling and mathematical computation as in reading, oral and written composition, and capacity for finding things out for themselves. They need less drill and less minute supervision in their work than do ordinary children, show more initiative, and can profitably use more freedom from class routine.

Various methods of catering to the needs of exceptional children are now in use in the high schools which furnished the information upon which the NEA bulletin is based. The most common and effective of these is sectioning classes on the basis of ability, giving to children in each group tasks suited to their capacity. This device is in use throughout our elementary and secondary school system. In some places it is very elaborately carried out. Three or more levels of ability are recognized and sometimes whole programs are provided in parallel, or honor schools are set up within the framework of a given high school. The effect of this division depends upon the extent to which it is carried out and upon the skill with which the work is varied to suit the needs of different groups. Obviously the grouping of pupils according to capacity is easier in large high schools than in small ones and it is much more common in the larger schools. One suspects from the illustrations given in the bulletin that teachers are often too modest in what they expect from the best groups. Some of the projects mentioned are excellent and cannot fail to carry the pupils further in their mastery of the subject; others seem largely futile and look like a kind of academic busy-work, time consuming but not rewarding in terms of educational advancement. An exception is found in Baltimore where selected students do the ordinary four-year college preparatory course in three years, devote the fourth to subjects usually studied in the Freshman class at college and upon graduation are regularly admitted to the Sophomore class in a number of colleges and universities.

Where separate classes and programs for students of different levels of ability are not thought to be feasible, superior students are sometimes given larger assignments in ordinary classes, or an attempt is made to offer them special opportunities for development in worth-while extra-curricular activities. The University of Nebraska offers supervised correspondence courses at the high-school level to pupils in that state in order to provide opportunities beyond the range of a given high-school faculty.

Exceptional pupils make much greater demands upon the school than the rank and file. They need better library facilities and better laboratory equipment. They make likewise more demands upon their teachers. On this point opinions of school principals as reflected in the bulletin are curiously divided. There is apparently much discussion throughout the country as to whether special teachers are needed for superior groups. This controversy, as the bulletin points out, does not go to the heart of the question. Superior pupils need less oversight than do those of average ability. They work more willingly and more independently, need less prodding, and are in that sense easier to teach. But the responsibility for bringing out the best in them is not on that account diminished. They need less drill, but more inspiration. Those qualities in a teacher which are desirable in teaching all children are needed in a higher degree for successful work with the best: high ability, sound scholarship and scholarly ambition, good health, freedom from envy, imagination, sympathy, and tact in dealing with individual problems. One would perhaps lay greater emphasis than do most principals upon the importance of thorough scholarship. Where the question is one of understanding and not of information, bright pupils of high-school age can understand the more advanced phases of a given subject better than mediocre college students. But they will not catch these vistas into the meaning and significance of any branch of knowledge unless the teacher is at home there, as no teacher can be who does not possess good ability plus sound scholarly training. Perhaps the one thing most needed to meet successfully this growing concern for the welfare of the best pupils in our secondary schools is increased emphasis upon scholarship in their teachers. Secondary work itself is delightful. To a certain type of individual it is far more attractive than college teaching. If instructors of this type, naturally fitted by their personal qualities to work with young pupils, were better trained, not by courses in education but by postgraduate work in their subject, they could be expected to do with their bright pupils things which less well-trained teachers can never accomplish.

The question whether sections of superior students should be taught by different teachers is beside the point. Obviously the qualities which make the teacher successful with superior students would make him or her successful with ordinary pupils as well, and if a given high school could be entirely staffed with teachers of such superior quality it would be so much the better place. Politically there are obvious advantages in not confining the work of the best teachers to the best pupils. Parents of pupils of ordinary ability are quite naturally and rightly concerned that their offspring should have the most favorable conditions and the best teaching the school can afford. Obviously the only completely satisfactory solution is to improve as far as possible all teaching for all pupils, giving to each those opportunities which his abilities enable him to use. It seems likely that no other solution will make it politically possible to develop a sound program for exceptional boys and girls in our public high-school system.

The question of public relations has already made difficulties in various cities where such programs have been attempted. Principals are divided on the question whether it is better to explain frankly the need and justification for an honors program or to say as little about it as possible. In some schools, sections of superior pupils are given some kind of neutral designation which it is hoped that the general public and even the pupils themselves will not understand, and attempts are made to play down the differences in the character of the work. Such attempts would in the nature of things seem to be doomed to failure. The problem can never be solved by bootlegging honors work. On the other hand some school systems have gone to the opposite extreme and indulge in publicity which, even if it does not threaten the continued existence of the honors plan, is certain to be extremely bad for the pupils concerned. One hears such terms as "genius section," and pupils are too frequently referred to as "intellectual prodigies." Nothing could be more unfortunate. Instead these brighter pupils should be led to think that it is only their duty to do the best work of which they are capable. It should be pointed out to them that there are many kinds of ability, of which theirs is only one. It should be assumed by parents and teachers alike that it is their duty to do their best. They should be kept humble by being led to compare themselves, not with average students in average classes, but with other individuals whose gifts correspond to their own. From top to bottom American education suffers from too much publicity and upon no group are the results of newspaper notoriety worse than upon students of high-school age.

For fifteen years the high schools of New York City have been interested in the provision of special opportunities for gifted pupils, and it has now come to be the established policy that such opportunities should be provided in every high school. After much experimentation the two devices most used are segregation of superior students in honors classes and the organization of special honors schools. In twenty-one schools, about which information is available, one or the other of these plans is in use; four have the system of separate honors classes, while seventeen have more or less fully developed honors schools, within the framework of the existing school organization. The curricula of these honors schools follow in general the lines prescribed for all students, but work is carried further and is more thoroughly done. Usually the college preparatory course is emphasized and in one or two honors schools it is prescribed.

The difference between honors classes and honors schools depends upon whether the special work provided for superior students affects only part of their program or all of it. Each high school has been allowed to develop its own procedure. Frequent surveys have been made of the work done, and there is constant lively discussion of suggestions for changes and improvements. This discussion has been in part reflected in some interesting articles in *High Points*, a monthly magazine published by the Board of Education for teachers in the high schools of New York City. A more careful and extended survey of the work done at the Evander Childs High School by Professor Lorge of Columbia is now in progress. One gathers from this discussion that while differences of opinion exist, interest and approval on the part of teachers, pupils, and their parents are constantly increasing. The proportion of pupils admitted to honors work runs from ten to twenty per cent. The policy is to enrich the programs of superior students rather than to accelerate their progress.

In the high schools of Baltimore superior students are allowed to take either an enriched course or an accelerated course, and more emphasis is placed upon the latter than is usual in high schools at the present time. At Baltimore City College, students who choose the accelerated plan take five courses per year instead of four and thus complete in four years the regular high school course, plus a substantial amount of work normally covered in the Freshman year at college. The advantages of such a plan are obvious, but certain Baltimore teachers feel that there are nevertheless disadvantages in that a student may be pushed too rapidly through work that could be better done in college. The question becomes one of teaching facilities and equipment. Since most elementary college work is actually of secondary school character— elementary English, mathematics, and foreign languages—it would seem that a case might be made for the high school as the place where work of this nature could most thoroughly be done.

Segregation of superior pupils in public high schools inevitably meets with opposition. The Roosevelt High School in Des Moines was selected by the school authorities as a kind of honors school, to which only the best would be admitted, but, much to the regret of the teaching staff, the plan had to be given up because of public opposition on the ground that this was undemocratic. In Denver another difficulty was experienced. The Eastern High School in that city was originally intended solely for pupils of high ability, but the plan was abandoned because of the difficulty experienced in identifying them. The surprising fact is not that such opposition should be encountered but that it has been in so many places successfully met and that the movement is spreading so rapidly.

While generalizations are dangerous, it is perhaps safe to say that the tendency of so-called progressive schools has been opposed to segregation of superior pupils. The effort has been instead to provide individualized instruction for all. At the Beaver Country Day School unusually able girls may be given more difficult assignments and be allowed to stay away from class during the period in which this work is being done. Courageous pupils in this school sometimes undertake very ambitious tasks on their own initiative, or at the suggestion of the teacher, and carry them successfully to completion.

The Eagle Rock High School in Los Angeles follows a similar policy. Both faculty and students believe that segregation of the best deprives all of valuable opportunities to learn social adjustment. Instead, superior students are given special responsibilities and opportunities within the regular program. This can doubtless more readily be done in a progressive school than in one more conventionally organized, but the fact remains that an increasing number of secondary-school teachers and principals believe that segregation of the best and the average into separate groups works to the advantage of both.

In private schools this policy of segregation is being more and more widely adopted. Good examples are Hotchkiss, George School, Culver, and Western Reserve Academy. At Hotchkiss the best groups do work which is far more advanced than would be possible for the average. At George School the language and science "sequences," to which only superior pupils are admitted, follow a program which calls for more individual initiative and represents a higher standard than the ordinary requirements for graduation. At Culver about half of all the courses are sectioned on the basis of ability and experimental honors seminars do admirable work, as do seminar groups at Western Reserve Academy. New endowments recently received by Lawrenceville and Phillips Exeter for individualized instruction have made possible the use of methods hitherto outside the reach of preparatory schools.

Gradually the crucial importance of secondary training is being realized. New resources are being placed at the disposal of schools; new methods are being tried and results undreamed of before are being achieved. The organization of work for superior students is as yet experimental and methods are rapidly changing. The problem of agreement upon uniform methods and standards, in so far as that is desirable, is a formidable one because of the number of schools and pupils involved and the variety of their clientèle. But problems of this character can be solved in spite of their difficulty. It is in secondary education that America lags furthest behind European standards, and it may easily happen that the next great improvement in American education will be made in this field.

Chapter Thirteen

HONORS WORK AND GRADUATE STUDY

'An unusually large proportion of honors graduates from Swarthmore, and I should expect from other colleges and universities as well, go on to postgraduate study. Swarthmore College has for many years kept in touch with its honors graduates, has collected reports from graduate schools about them, and has received reports from the students themselves on their experience. It is to be expected that these individuals would make good records in advanced work and the facts go beyond what could have been expected. The effect of their training in preparing them for independent study and research has been noted by their teachers everywhere. The careful organization of honors work at Swarthmore has meant that the young graduate begins with a better knowledge of his chosen field than the student whose choice of undergraduate courses has been more haphazard. Honors graduates, in some cases, where the regulations of a particular graduate school permitted, have been able to dispense with some of the course work usually required for the Ph.D. degree.[1]

The comments of Swarthmore honors graduates on the way in which their experience in honors work did, or did not, prepare them for graduate study are full of interest. Before

[1] The following paragraphs are quoted by permission from a paper read at the thirty-seventh annual conference of the Association of American Universities at Cornell in 1935 and published in their proceedings.

summarizing these comments, however, I must point out that (honors work is not designed primarily as a preparation for graduate work but rather as a discipline leading to a better liberal education, and that its primary justification is and should be on that basis.) Swarthmore graduates would be the first to say that, and, indeed, have said it in their letters. "I received from honors work intellectual training and discipline which are valuable in their own right," is one comment. "It gave me work to do which will probably interest me the rest of my life," is another. A third graduate says:

In my opinion, the advantages of honors work are, to a large extent, identical, whether the honors student expects at the end of his course to take up graduate study or to enter business or a profession.

A fourth writes:

The value of honors work, over and above the preparation for later study, is synonymous with its value as a liberal educa-tion. . . . Instead of getting his education in small and probably sterilized doses in which he sees little intrinsic value, the honors student is inspired with a vital interest in intellectual and artistic fields and learns how to work in them independently. After he leaves college he will quite naturally continue in the cultural life introduced to him by honors work, whereas the course student will probably lose a great deal of the cultural interest he got in college because it was less spontaneous and more dependent on instruction.

One man, who has left graduate school to go into business, has this to say about his training:

The real value of the honors system, in my case, lay in the tendency it inspired to a habit of self-help and individual thinking. I felt a noticeable advantage in this respect at graduate school, and have been engaged in a type of business—the buying department of the investment banking business—calling for critical and exhaustive analysis, not of securities so much as of industries, companies as "going concerns," and management. In this work the training received through the honors method of study has, in my opinion, been invaluable.

(Perhaps a part of the usefulness of honors work as a preparation for graduate study lies precisely in the fact that the emphasis is upon liberal training, and the tendency, therefore, is to produce liberal scholarship.) One young man, who has already made a promising start on a scholarly career, expresses very strongly that opinion in a letter which I shall quote a little later.

The training offered under the honors plan seems to Swarthmore graduates a good liberal education, because of the great interest it arouses, because they discover for themselves the pleasures of study, and become excited about learning. A good deal of the intensity of honors work proceeds, I am sure, from the stimulus of close, informal contact between student and professor. Under the honors plan, individual guidance is not a mere supplement to class work. The seminar is the principal method of teaching, and it is the lectures and classes which are incidental. This contact with members of the faculty overcomes, as one student has pointed out, the characteristic carelessness and indifference of the undergraduate. It gives to academic work the driving power of personal association and admiration. The development of intellectual interests becomes for the students concerned, during four undergraduate years, perhaps not the sole, but certainly the main, business of life, and it is not surprising that they learn to do their best. It is precisely this drive which is needed to carry a man through the drudgery which the difficult ideal of exact scholarship demands; with this impulse the most laborious scholarship remains humane. The whole matter was well put by one classical honors student, now engaged on a piece of research which involves an unusual amount of what must be called scholastic drudgery:

In my own particular case I have found that I might conceivably have entered graduate work with a more thorough preparation in the classical languages and literatures. It would not be fair, however, to ascribe all of this deficiency to honors work. My own interests, which tend to the historical rather than to the philological or literary study of classical times, would in any case have made some such deficiency inevitable.

Over against this deficiency, which may be regarded as having been in some degree fostered by the freedom allowed me in honors work, I have to set the memory of an intellectual experience and a training in clear and balanced thinking so inspiring that even the present fourth year of graduate work with constant study of minutiae of the (frequently) driest sort cannot erase it. Without such a preliminary training of a non-technical nature I am in some doubt whether the specialization I am now carrying out would be at all supportable, and in any case the rationale of my present studies has been made clearer to me than it could have been otherwise.

The experience of honors work seems to these undergraduates a good liberal training, furthermore, because of the freedom in which they do their work, because of the scope it offers for intellectual initiative and independence, because they take a large share of responsibility for their own education and depend not upon the prodding of a teacher, but upon their own courage and self-reliance. This "more adult and more imaginative experience," as one student called it, sharpens and matures their minds as mere classroom drill would not. This "freedom from the time-wasting requirements of class attendance, monthly quizzes, credit-grade-hour demands, and, more important, freedom from the psychological emphasis on

secondary or irrelevant goals which these requirements in-
spire" is mentioned in every comment. The honors student
learns to plan for himself, to budget his time, to work toward
a distant goal.

Swarthmore graduates believe, for the reasons given above,
that honors work is a good preparation for graduate study
because they get from it a good liberal education. In addition
to this, they believe themselves better prepared for the specific
tasks of postgraduate work than their fellows who have been
trained under the conventional course and hour plan, partly
because of the grasp which they get of their particular fields
of knowledge, and partly because of their training in methods
of work.

I shall consider factual preparation first, because it is upon
this side of the training that critics of honors work are most
likely to fasten, and it is in this respect that I find a certain
difference of opinion among Swarthmore graduates, corresponding, I think, to a difference in the organization of honors
work in various subjects. In this respect variation of practice
between departments at Swarthmore is pretty wide. Some
give to their honors students an excellent mastery of many
of the subjects ordinarily reserved for the graduate school;
others leave for graduate study some subjects ordinarily taken
in the undergraduate course. It is clear that in matters of this
kind there is room for legitimate difference of opinion.

On the whole it would be fair to say that most Swarthmore
honors graduates report that the ground they have covered
anticipates a part, or all, of the first year of graduate work. In
many cases they are excused from some of the courses ordinarily required, and hardly need the usual three years for the
Ph.D. For example:

Honors work at Swarthmore was very satisfactory training for graduate study here. It was possible, due to the training received, to enter directly the field of research instead of spending the usual year of graduate work in courses, since these courses had been covered in the undergraduate work at Swarthmore.

Many others report the same experience.

On the other hand, some find themselves less well prepared than they would like. For example, neither Latin nor Anglo-Saxon is required for the honors course in English, and the department has laid more emphasis upon the understanding and appreciation of literature and the thorough and thoughtful study of major authors than upon "covering the ground" in period courses of the survey type. A good case can be made for this kind of preparation. For the students who are not going on to graduate study, it is excellent; among other things, it gives them the impulse to read for themselves. Those who do enter graduate work often express themselves as in sympathy with this approach, even though it makes it necessary for them to cover in graduate school ground that might have been covered in college. One English honors student, whose experience was precisely this, makes the following comment:

The honors work in English was definitely not a pre-graduate course, and as such was much more valuable than the extensive survey courses in literature and linguistics would be. Inasmuch as the emphasis was upon the interpretative rather than the scholarly approach to literature, I should say that my experience in honors work was supplementary to graduate work rather than a direct preparation for it.

I think that it would be a mistake to change the work too much in the direction of pre-graduate study. Graduate work presupposes a taste for literature, and an ability to interpret it. This, I feel, is the function of honors work, a function which can best be fulfilled by the honors method.

The degree to which the Swarthmore graduate feels handicapped varies, of course, with the requirements of the various graduate schools. When history or philosophy may be substituted for philology, the difficulties disappear, since Swarthmore English majors usually choose these subjects as minors in honors work.

To some extent, the adequacy of factual preparation in all subjects lies within the choice of the individual student. He may, by his selection of minors, build up his knowledge in a relatively limited field, or he may range somewhat more widely if he prefers. Such decisions are difficult for students in choosing and for the faculty in determining within just what limits choice should be allowed. I may say that, on the whole, the Swarthmore faculty has leaned toward the side of thoroughness in the mastery of a limited field, with the result that the great majority of our graduates find their factual training adequate and even generous. Students may regret the limitations imposed in the interests of thoroughness, even though they recognize at the same time that it is worth the price. One says:

I do often regret that honors work limited me so much to purely scientific subjects. I would like to have been able to obtain a more general knowledge of liberal arts. However, I realize one cannot take everything he desires in four short years. I did learn one subject well, and in that honors work did a lot for me.

It is my opinion that the concentration of a student's work upon one field is not a narrowing process, provided his intellectual curiosity remains active enough to lead him to desire constantly to range further afield as opportunity offers. The point is well made in a letter from another student, which I quote:

I should say that this sense of relative values . . . is the chief importance of honors work over and above its worth as a preparation for advanced study. Delving into a limited division instead of scattering one's energy over many unrelated fields is far from being a narrowing process. For the further one delves in one field, the more its relations with other fields are realized. This knowledge that the boundary lines between the various branches are unimportant is supplemented by many informal discussions with students majoring in various divisions. The discussions begun in seminars have a way of carrying over into the dormitory and being pursued long after the seminar. In this way one becomes interested in fields other than one's own, and the eagerness to learn more about them is still felt after graduation.

I find my own belief in the value of doing a limited task well is borne out by the experience of a few Swarthmore students who have done graduate work in subjects quite different from the ones they studied in college. In such a case the students have, of course, most of the elements of their new specialties still to master. Nevertheless, they report that they do this with ease and even, it seems to them, more readily than other students trained in conventional courses in the subject itself. The mastery of one field by methods of independent work gives the individual a training which enables him to make rapid and effective progress in dealing with other and quite different subject matter.

On the other side of the preparation for graduate study, in training in methods of work, in the development of intellectual enthusiasm, in sharpening the critical faculties, the value of honors work seems to Swarthmore graduates absolutely clear, and nothing could increase the strength of their endorsement of it. They are naturally curious about their own preparation as compared with that of students who have come up to graduate school through the conventional course and hour plan. Swarthmore graduates are convinced that the training they get in honors work is superior. They all say so, and offer many interesting illustrations of the point. For example one graduate writes:

I am delighted to express an opinion on honors work. My opportunities for reflection on the system have been a little unusual. My sister entered another college, in which the honors system was not used, at the same time that I entered Swarthmore. For four years we pursued similar courses. She was a brilliant student and graduated at the top of her class. We spent most of our week-ends together so that we had every opportunity to compare our progress. There is no doubt in either of our minds that my last two years reading for honors gave me a decided advantage in independence of thought, in discussion, in correlation of subject matter, and in comprehension of educational technique.

Honors students have become accustomed to the use of sources, to finding their own references, to the organization of material; they have already served a kind of apprenticeship in scholarly work. They report that their training stands them in especially good stead in thesis work and research, which are the parts of graduate study which they most enjoy and in which they most excel. The liberal emphasis in their undergraduate training leads them instinctively to do more than accumulate facts, leads them to integrate details into a coherent whole, and to seek to understand their significance. Reading between the lines of the letters which they write, it seems clear to me that this plan of study sends students into research with more perspective and a truer sense of relative values than would ordinarily be the case where an individual had not had the opportunity of surveying a limited field of knowledge for himself.

A second point, mentioned in many letters, is the habit of critical analysis of conclusions as over against mere learning of facts. Certainly this is the ideal of all teaching, and it is an ideal which I am convinced honors work turns into a reality. The following comment on this point is typical of many others:

I know that for me the most important and significant factor in reading for honors was the method. Probably its most fundamental contribution was a habit of thought; treating all material that came before the mind as the basis for thinking and reasoning, instead of merely accepting facts and opinions and conclusions as static, to be learned and eventually, in good part, forgotten. I believe that the seminar method, the close contact with fellow students and professors, is directly responsible for such mental training. The ability and willingness to discuss a point cogently and without embarrassment, and to stand up under criticism, to look for criticism eagerly, also comes out of the method of group study.

A third specific point insisted upon by every individual was the value of learning to work independently, to rely upon one's own efforts. Honors work has largely increased the demands upon the library at Swarthmore, and graduates speak with the keenest appreciation of the opportunities they enjoy in this direction in the great universities. This point is brought out in all of their letters. They tend to treat their courses not as an end in themselves, but rather as a point of departure for individual reading and research.

As a veteran of many years' experience in the teaching of English composition, I have been extraordinarily interested to see the effect of honors work on the way in which students write and speak. As the honors program has developed at Swarthmore, formal training in English composition has come to have a smaller and smaller place, and many students get none at all. On the other hand, visitors to honors seminars continually ask how it is that students are taught to write so well. They are, of course, picked students, and superior individuals use better English, on the whole, whether specifically trained in it or not. Furthermore, they write a great deal for their seminars, and since their papers will be read and critically discussed, in many cases for style as well as for content, they try to make them as effective as they can. Certainly their papers sound well when read in seminars. They are natural, spontaneous, and not self-conscious, but sometimes careless as to structure; they have the strength and the weakness of writing which is intended to be read aloud. The merits of such writing are great, but its defects are real. The whole problem is one which requires constant vigilance, but it seems that the efforts of professors in various departments produce more effect than would a similar amount of work spent in the teaching of "pure" composition.

Seminars train students not merely to write but also to talk. The keen discussion which takes place in them is perhaps the most valuable single part of the honors discipline. These discussions last interminably, and, as the student whom I quoted indicates, are frequently prolonged after the seminar is over, in the dormitories in the evening after dinner. Rhodes Scholars, in comparing their Oxford experience with the life in their own American universities, are likely to envy most the interesting, light-hearted, unpedantic talk about serious subjects, of which the English undergraduate is so fond. Honors work has produced a similar effect at Swarthmore, and certainly, as a means of mental training, it is of inestimable value.

So far as I can judge, the opinion which Swarthmore students themselves hold of the value of their training as a preparation for higher study is borne out by the opinions expressed by their honors examiners and by their professors in graduate schools. I have not, however, undertaken to supplement the statements of these students by any similar inquiry addressed to professors and deans of graduate schools. In one way or another a large number of such comments have come back to the College. They are overwhelmingly favorable and enormously reassuring. I omit them, however, from this chapter, partly because they do not come from any orderly inquiry, and it would be natural that any unfavorable opinions which graduate professors might hold of the merits of Swarthmore students would be slower to come back to the College authorities. I omit them, in the second place, because on this particular point I think the students are better authorities than their graduate school professors would be. In the nature of things, it might be difficult for a teacher in a graduate school to distinguish, in the case of one of his good students, how much of that superiority was due to undergraduate preparation and how much of it was due to the excellence of the training of the particular graduate school. On the other hand, the student will know, and his evidence on that point is better than any other.

From Swarthmore graduates and from Rholes Scholars who have taken the American Ph.D. following an honors degree at Oxford, I have heard for many years criticisms of the rigidity of the course requirements for the doctor's degree in our graduate schools. Normally these required courses fill up two of the three years which the graduate student is expected to spend in work for his degree. Often the courses differ very little in character from undergraduate work. Their purpose is to give the student such a general familiarity with his special field as he ought to get from a well-organized undergraduate course of honors quality. This work is tested by a series of general examinations, taken usually at the end of the second year of graduate work, following which the student is allowed to enter upon research and the writing of his thesis.

Some graduate schools are flexible as regards course requirements, relaxing them for students whose preparation has been better, and depending upon the general examination to test the student's readiness to begin research. But in many graduate schools rigidity is the rule. Students who are eager to begin research are held to a large number of petty course requirements and denied any opportunity of demonstrating by examination that for them this drudgery is unnecessary.

(An immense improvement could be made in the work of graduate schools if students were given a clear outline or syllabus of the field to be covered by way of general background and if they were then allowed more freedom in the time and method of preparation for the examinations by which their knowledge is tested.)No relaxation is called for in the severity of the general examinations. The standard should be kept as high as at present or might be made higher. But the student should be given more freedom as to the method of preparation and the time spent in preparation for them. The success of the honors plan throughout the country indicates that the best students would make good use of such freedom, would be happier in independent work, and would produce better results than can be attained by rigid course requirements. In some graduate schools this practice is followed with notable success. That it has not become the rule in all is probably due to the poor preparation with which many graduate students begin their advanced work.

The probabilities are that a freer method of preparation for general examinations would operate to shorten the time which the best graduate students would have to give to this part of their work and would correspondingly lengthen the time which they would be able to devote to the thesis. This would be a great improvement. The Ph.D. in this country at present is too much a matter of taking courses and accumulating credit hours and depends too little upon research. The standard of quality of the research done should be made higher and the writer of an unsatisfactory thesis should be refused his degree. As it is, students fail frequently in the general examination, rarely on the thesis, not because the work done for the one is poorer, but because faculties are more insistent on what the student learns at second hand than upon what he does for himself. If the method of preparation for the general examination were more independent, the type of student who succeeded best under this freer method would be the type most likely to succeed in research.

Furthermore a more flexible system of preparation for the general examinations for the Ph.D. would inevitably make these examinations more of a test of ability than they are at present. It is important that students who are preparing for research should have covered the field in which they expect to work: it is still more important that they be men and women of unusual ability. So long as the general examinations are based primarily upon preparation in required courses, the first element, ground covered, will tend to be emphasized as against the second qualification of individual ability. The doctor's degree would mean more if, without relaxing the standard for the first, more emphasis were placed upon the latter qualification. Abler students would welcome the increased freedom and increased demand upon their own intellectual initiative and independence, while weaker students would be discouraged by what to them would be a more severe requirement and thus some misfits might be deflected to other careers where their chances of success would be greater.

In such ways the regulations for the doctor's degree might well be modified in accordance with the experience of American colleges and universities in the administration of honors work. For the Ph.D. no division between honors and pass students is called for. If the doctor's degree means anything it should mean that all the individuals who take it are of honors caliber. What is called for is that they should be treated as honors students are treated, left more upon their own responsibility, to succeed or fail, without spoon-feeding or meticulous course requirements.

Such an alteration in the regime of our graduate schools would place more emphasis on research. That is greatly to be desired. The value of the degree would be immensely improved if two years instead of one were ordinarily allowed for the writing of the thesis and if the standard for the thesis, both as to content and as to form, were correspondingly higher. One hears nowadays a good deal of comment in the opposite direction. It is argued that, in preparation for teaching, research is largely irrelevant and that candidates would be better prepared if more attention were bestowed upon their mastery of the available knowledge in their field of study. This point of view seems to me to run directly counter to the best interests of American higher education. I have already indicated that honors students are most effectively taught by professors who are themselves creative scholars. Any change which would emphasize the element of research in the preparation for the Ph.D. would, I am convinced, better prepare the holders of that degree to be useful leaders of the best undergraduate students.

After the First World War the doctor's degree was instituted at both Oxford and Cambridge out of deference to

American opinion and in order to satisfy American demands. It was not thought at the time that there would be many English candidates for the degree, but this expectation, I may say in passing, has not been borne out in practice. The degree has thoroughly justified itself for its value in meeting the needs of English students, and the majority of the candidates are not American but English.

It is the fashion in Oxford and Cambridge to lament the lack of "organization" of their work for the Ph.D. The standards for admission to candidacy for the degree are high—ordinarily a first or a good second in an honor school. The standards for the degree itself are also high and candidates for it frequently fail. But once a man is admitted to candidacy for the degree he is left largely to his own devices. He must present a thesis which, in the opinion of his examiners, makes a significant contribution to knowledge, and he must show in his examination an adequate grasp of the accepted knowledge of that field. One or more of his examiners will be persons who have had no part in his training.

In the preparation of his thesis the student has the benefit of the advice of a supervisor, who stands ready to help him in any way requested, but who does not take responsibility for his success. Much more than in the United States, the student is left to his own devices, and must take the responsibility for his own success or failure. It might well be argued that the lack of organization and detailed requirements, so often lamented, lends to the training for the doctor's degree in England its greatest value. Certain it is that Rhodes Scholars who have taken the Oxford D.Phil. and American students who have received the corresponding Ph.D. at Cambridge have been notably successful as scholars and teachers in the United States after their return. By comparison, the American Ph.D. is too narrowly supervised, too much schoolmastered, and is made too easy for the mediocre candidate. Especially does it lack adequate scope for the exercise of individual initiative and independence, qualities which are so important in intellectual work and which are so well developed under the various honors plans described in this volume. From those plans our graduate schools could gather many useful hints for making the Ph.D. a sounder training than it is for the abler and more resourceful student.

INDEX

Activities, extra-curricular, effect on honors work 127, 132-4; opportunity for initiative 14-15; at Swarthmore, 43

Administration of honors work, 124 ff

Agnes Scott College, 55

American, British and Continental Universities compared, 26-7

Amherst College, 66

Associate in Arts degree, 98, 104-5

Association of American Universities, approved list, 45, 102, 103

Athletics and honors work, 121, 132-4; at Swarthmore, 43

Aydelotte, Frank, "Honors courses at Swarthmore," 44 (note); Inaugural address, 31-2; National Research Council report on honors work, vii (note); *The Oxford Stamp*, 24 (note); *Oxford of Today*, 22 (note); "Progress of the American College," 28 (note); "The University System at Michigan," 48 (note); "What the American Rhodes Scholar Gets from Oxford," 27 (note)

Bates College, 66

Baltimore High Schools, facilities for superior pupils, 154, 158

Beaver Country Day School, treatment of superior pupils, 159

Beloit College, 66

Blanshard, Brand, Syllabus for Moral Philosophy, 111-12

Blanshard, Frances B., x

Boston College, 75, 88, 142; use of external examiners, 119

Boston University, 66

Bowdoin College, 49

Branscomb, B. H., needs and functions of college libraries, 137

Breadth, misconception of in American education, 131

Brooks, Robert C., 32; *Reading for Honors at Swarthmore*, 44 (note)

Brown University, 59

Bryn Mawr College, 60

Buffalo University of, 50

California, University of, 96, 97

Carnegie Corporation, appropriation for inspection of honors work, viii, ix, x

Chattanooga, University of, use of external examiners, 119

Chicago College Plan, 50-2, 142, 144, 145, 146

Clark University, 66

Classics of the Western World, influence on American higher education, 68, 69 (note)

Colgate University, 49-50

College Entrance Examination Board, 148-9

College of the City of New York, 64

Colorado, University of, 95

Columbia University, 48, 68-70

Comprehensive Examinations, 117-23; at Swarthmore, 37

Crosby, L. A., Editor, *Oxford of Today*, 22 (note)

DATE DUE

OCT 13 2004			
			Printed in USA